The Peking Massacre
A Summary Report of the 1989 Democracy Movement In Mainland China

Published by Kwang Hwa Publishing Company
2, Tientsin Street, Taipei, (Taiwan), ROC

Printed by China Art Printing Works Yu Tai Industrial Corp., Ltd.
6, Pao-chiang Rd., Hsin-tien, Taipei Hsien, Taiwan, ROC.

1st edition, D 5   July 1989
Catalog Card No.: KHP-EN-BO-78-043-78I
ISBN 957-9227-00-4

Printed in the Republic of China on Taiwan

Price: NT$80   US$4.00

Introduction

The people of mainland China have long been persecuted under the Communist regime. They, especially the students and intellectuals, realize that forty years of communist rule have brought political dictatorship, inflation, and widespread abuse of privilege. Consequently, in April 1989, on the occasion of the mourning rites for the late General Secretary of the Central Committee of the Chinese Communist Party, Hu Yao-pang, they launched an explosive democracy movement, which lasted altogether over fifty days and was ended temporarily by the brutal, bloody suppression of the Chinese Communists.

According to various reports, the students and people killed or wounded by indiscriminate machine gun fire from Communist troops or crushed by tanks numbered in the several thousands. This tragic event, the like of which is rarely seen in the world, drew not only grief but massive condemnation from the people of the world.

In order to set the record straight regarding this wound of history, this publishing company has specially assembled various historical materials and edited this special publication, to inform people from all walks of life about the whole story and truth of the Peking massacre. At the same time, we express our sincere grief for the martyrs at Tienanmen Square who gave their lives for freedom and democracy and wish good fortune to those in mainland China still struggling for democracy, hoping that they may soon enjoy free and happy lives.

Table of Contents

The Peking Massacre: A Summary Report of
the 1989 Democracy Movement in Mainland China 1
    I. The Democracy Movement: Its Beginning and Development
    II. Causes of the Democracy Movement
    III. An Intense and Sharp Response
    IV. Effects of the Democracy Movement

A Statement by the Government of the
Republic of China, on the Movement for Freedom
and Democracy in Mainland China..................................19
    May 21, 1989

Statement on the Situation in Mainland China.................21
    Lee Teng-hui, President, Republic of China, June 4, 1989

Press Release of the Government Information
Office, Executive Yuan 23
    June 4, 1989

Statement by the ROC Government in Regard to
the Continued Killings by the Chinese Communists
of Supporters of the Democracy Movement
in Mainland China..25
    June 22, 1989

Illustrations 27

The Peking Massacre
A Summary Report of the 1989 Democracy Movement In Mainland China

I. The Democracy Movement: Its Beginning and Development

On April 15, 1989, former Secretary-General of the Central Committee of the Chinese Communist Party and Politburo member Hu Yao-pang died of a heart attack. His death was announced that afternoon. The next day, crowds of students and residents of Peking laid wreaths at the Monument to the People's Heroes at Tienanmen Square to honor Hu. News coverage of activities at Tienanmen Square by the official *People's Daily* drew even more people to the square, leading to the largest popular movement in mainland China.

By April 17, the crowd at Tienanmen had grown to significant proportions, with many people carrying funeral banners, elegiac couplets, sheets, and big character posters, which attracted larger crowds. On April 18th, students from several universities and colleges in Peking staged a sit-in in front of the Great Hall of the People and presented a seven-point petition to the Chinese Communist authorities. Their petition consisted of the following demands:

1. To reassess Hu Yao-pang's record.

2. To renounce completely movements to "Eliminate Spiritual Pollution" and to "Oppose Bourgeois Liberalization."

3. Freedom of the press and an end to the newspaper bans.

4. To order party chiefs and their children to disclose their income and property holdings.

5. To increase the budget for education and raise the salaries of intellectuals.

6. To lift the ban on marches and demonstrations in Peking.

7. To allow the press to cover properly the demonstrations and student sit-in at Tienanmen.

As students continued to turn out in large numbers to demonstrate and express their dissatisfaction with the government, the mood of protest grew more intense. Hu's funeral on April 22 attracted over 100,000 students and ordinary people, who marched and chanted slogans calling for freedom and democracy. Students from several universities then started boycotting classes. Similar demonstration activities occurred in Sian, Shanghai, Nanking, Canton, Hangchow, and other major cities, with violent confrontations being reported in some areas. On April 23, the communist authorities brought 20,000 troops to Peking, but the students and the masses still continued their protests.

In its strongly-worded editorial of April 26, the *People's Daily* unabashedly pointed out the "necessity of a clear-cut stand opposing this chaos." By labelling the student democracy movement "chaos," the *People's Daily* provoked intense dissatisfaction among the students, who viewed demonstrations as a legal right granted by the constitution, and not as "chaos" as termed by the Chinese Communists. As a result, on April 27, close to 200,000 people broke through army and police lines and marched into Tienanmen Square, where they staged a sit-in as a way to lodge their protest and to press their demand for a "dialogue" with communist leaders. After two days of delaying, the Communist Party's Central Committee sent State Council spokesman Yuan Mu and several others to open a dialogue with the student leaders. Yuan Mu and his aides, however, did not accept any of the students' demands, but instead sought to lecture them. This further enraged the students, provoking even larger demonstrations. This period coincided with the 70th anniversary of the May Fourth Movement, a movement for democracy and science. On May 4 the students organized a rally with over 300,000 participants, in which members of the official news media also participated. Demonstrations also took place in Shanghai, Nanking, and Canton in support of the Peking movement, which marked another high point in the democracy movement. By May 9, over 1,000 members of the official news organs, including reporters and editors from the *People's Daily*, the *New China News Agency*, and more than 30 newspapers and broadcasting organizations, had taken part in marches and rallies calling for greater freedom of the press. This combination of students and media personnel lent further momentum to the movement.

The movement entered a new stage when 2,000 students staged a hunger strike on May 13. The number of hunger strikers soon swelled to 3,000, and the people of Peking were moved by their plight, prompting a demonstration by one million people on May 17. The number doubled to two million the next day, while demonstrations in support of the democracy movement took place in over 30 other cities and regions. The massive scale and tremendous momentum of these demonstrations were the high tide of the movement, which stunned the entire world.

The Chinese Communists, seeing that the situation had almost gotten completely out of hand, on May 20 declared martial law in parts of Peking, clamped down on the media, and brought in troops from different parts of the mainland to surround Peking. Residents of Peking blocked major roads to prevent the troops from entering the city, and the infuriated communist authorities accused the students of fermenting anarchy.

By May 28 the momentum of the large-scale mass movement had ebbed somewhat. Different opinions about whether or not to stay in Tienanmen surfaced among the students, but they finally agreed to stay until June 20, the date of the first meeting of the Standing Committee of the National People's Congress. At this time only about 10,000 students still remained in the square, and the democracy movement seemed to lack the strength to carry on. However, two days later students of the Peking Institute of the Arts erected a 10-meter statue of the "Goddess of Democracy" on the square, again attracting a crowd of more than 100,000 people.

On June 2, singer Hou Te-chien and three others began a hunger strike in Tienanmen in support of the students, attracting a crowd of 500,000, but there were already signs that the Chinese Communists would resort to armed suppression. In the early morning of June 3, pushing and shoving matches broke out between the people of Peking and the army seeking to enter the city. As the hour drew late, tens of thousands of communist troops, led by armored personnel carriers and tanks, finally attacked Tienanmen from six directions, launching the bloody suppression. Troops entered the city and attacked the students, first with tear gas and later with tanks and machine guns. Tanks and armored personnel carriers charged into the crowds, raking machine gun fire. The people fought back with stones and Molotov cocktails. The casualties numbered in the thousands. After several hours of indiscriminate killing, the troops succeeded in clearing Tienanmen Square. Soldiers continued to chase after fleeing citizens, shooting some as they tried to escape into alleys and lanes leading away from the square. Peking residents reacted with shock and anger, and many came out into the streets to denounce the soldiers as "fascists" and "mad killers." They were answered with further rounds of machine gun fire.

News of the bloodbath at Tienanmen soon spread to other cities and drew reactions of rage. Violent confrontations increased as tens of thousands of people took part in marches in Shanghai, Nanking, Canton, Changsha, Wuhan, Lanchow, Hangchow, Chengtu, Sian, and Tientsin to protest the massacre. On June 5, residents of Peking continued to wage street battles against troops of the People's Liberation Army, which deployed large numbers of tanks and helicopters to quell the resistance. Soldiers fired indiscriminately with automatic weapons at civilians and innocent bystanders. To stop news of the carnage from reaching the outside world, the Communist authorities forbade foreign journalists from interviewing people, and ordered that all news dispatches be reviewed before release.

People everywhere in China were furious. On June 6, a group of people in Shanghai laid themselves across railway tracks in protest to stop a Shanghai-bound train. The train crushed them, and over 40 people were killed or injured in the crash. Angry crowds beat up policemen at the scene and set the train afire. Faced with massive unrest in major cities after the Peking massacre, the Communist authorities responded by using armed force to suppress the people.

On the day when the bloodshed took place in Tienanmen Square and the following days as unrest continued, there were many sad and moving scenes.

—While a column of tanks was heading to continue its mission of suppression elsewhere, an unarmed citizen courageously stood in front of them, with the imposing manner of one guarding a pass against an army of 10,000. The tanks tried several times to move forward, but the man did not flinch. The desperate impasse between the hero and the tanks lasted more than half an hour. To those who saw the scene on television, the hero's indomitable resolution truly defeated the might of the tanks.

—The arm of a dead young man was found with his address in his hometown written upon it. The man must have decided that he would be willing to sacrifice even his own life for the democracy movement. With the address on his arm, his body could be taken back to his native place, just as in the Chinese expression, "The fallen leaf returns to its roots."

—In a hospital in Peking, a Peking University professor was in a critical condition with bullet and bayonet wounds. But he refused painkiller injections, saying, "I am going to die. This country will perish. The Chinese Communists have lied to us. It's meaningless for me to stay in this world. Please tell my wife to take care of our baby." The baby was only two months old.

—While facing armed police 300 meters away, an old professor at the Academy of Sciences of China said impassionedly to his four students with tears in his eyes, "In my whole life I only said one thing wrong—once I shouted with others the slogan 'Long live the Chinese Communist Party!'"

—In Peking, in many ceremonies mourning the deaths of the democracy movement students, elegiac couplets such as "martyr to the national cause," "A blood debt will be paid by blood," "The land is stained with blood—a rare tragedy on earth" and balls made of white flowers were hung in every mourning hall. Some people even wore mourning clothes for the dead.

—Gunshot wounds could be seen on the bodies of many youngsters and civilians. Some had one, some two or three, and there were still others with several wounds.

—Perhaps having decided early that there would be severe suppression, Yang Shang-kun said in an emergency meeting on the night of June 4: "Don't be afraid of people being killed. Even if 100,000 in Peking are killed, let alone 1,000 or 2,000, it doesn't matter. So many people have been killed, now we cannot retreat but only advance."

Immediately, Peking—a city of ancient cultural heritage, was permeated by an atmosphere of desolation, terror and grief. Even more pitiful, Yuan Mu, the spokesman of the State Council said that only 23 students had died, but that more than 300 soldiers had been killed, whereas innumerable bodies of students and civilians could be clearly seen, sacrifices of the cruel tragedy.

Teng Hsiao-ping, the actual leader of the Chinese Communists, appeared in public on June 9. He praised the Chinese Communist army for stopping the "counter-revolutionary riot," and ordered a hunt for the leaders of the democracy movement and students. The students, on the other hand, said they would break into scattered groups, and go underground to continue their advocacy of democracy. An explosive movement for democracy seems to have been halted, yet it has not ended, but has only entered a new phase.

Unfortunately, a frightening wave of arrests has already begun, ordered by Chinese Communist premier Li Peng. Mass media reports indicate that Li has ordered the arrest of 20,000 people. The atomsphere of a "great clean-up" and a "great purge" accordingly has plunged the people of Peking into a state of insecurity and terror. On June 13, warrants for the arrests of 21 leaders of the democracy movement were issued by the public security agencies of the Chinese Communists. The wanted are Wang Dan, Liu Kang, Yang Tao, Feng Tsung-teh, Wang Yu-tsai, Chang Po-li, and Hsiung Yen from Peking University; Wu'er Kai-hsi, Chai Ling, and Liang Ching-tun (Liang Chao-erh) from Peking Teachers University; Chou Feng-chen, Chang Ming, and Hsiung Wei from Tsinghua University; Wang Chih-hsi and Chang Chih-ching from China University of Political Science and Law; Chai Wei-min from the Peking Institute of Economics; Wang Cheng-yun from the Central Institute of Nationalities; Cheng Hsu-kuang from the Peking Aeronautical Institute; Ma Shao-fang from the Peking Film Academy; Wang Chao-hua from the Postgraduate Institute under the Academy of Social Sciences of China; and Li Lu from Nanking University.

Since the issue of the arrest warrants, people one after the other have met with misfortune. By the end of June, a total of 1,700 had been arrested throughout the mainland, with 33 having been executed. Arrests continue to mount, and the atmosphere of terror intensifies. A new storm of bloodshed has been launched on the Chinese mainland, and even more lamentably, the people, the physique, and the future of mainland China, will all be devastated by this tremendous storm.

II. Causes of the Democracy Movement

From the beginning, the actions of the democracy demonstrators were moderate and rational, and their appeals consistent. Up until the eve of the massacre on June 4th, the demands of the people had not gone beyond those seven points raised by the students sitting in on April 18th, which can be summarized as struggling for freedom and democracy, anti-corruption, and better treatment of intellectuals.

This protest movement, started by university students in Peking, quickly won the sympathy and support of people from all classes and areas, who in turn responded in kind. The problems raised by the students clearly had worsened to a point where the people could tolerate them no longer, evolving finally into the eruption of a large-scale, popular movement. These problems are worth examining in detail:

1. The Chinese Communists have done their utmost to reject democracy: the Chinese Communists have consistently clung to their feudal idea of "conquer the domain; sit and enjoy all from it," and have stubbornly clung to power, unwilling to allow the people to

be master of their own house. The efforts of the intellectuals in their struggle for democracy already span several decades, from their opposition to communist dictatorship in 1956, the big character poster, "On the Socialist Democratic Legal System," by Li Yi-che in 1974, "The Fifth Modernization—Political Democratization" of Wei Ching-sheng in 1978, "The Nineteen Point Declaration of Chinese Human Rights" drafted by Jen Wan-ting in the "Peking Spring" in 1979, to the student mass movement for freedom and democracy at the end of 1986 and beginning of 1987. For several decades, these calls for democracy have risen one after the other, all being suppressed completely by the Chinese Communists. At the beginning of 1987, after Hu Yao-pang was forced to step down, the Chinese Communists, to show their determination to oppose democracy, went so far as to launch the "Anti-bourgeois Liberalization" movement to attack those who were struggling for and advocating democracy. For over ten years, intellectuals had ceaselessly struggled for democracy, but had not received support from the general public, and so were unable to broaden and converge their influence. This time, however, as the students again launched a democracy movement, the public clearly understood that democracy was closely related to their own personal lives and interests. They did not sit and watch, but joined the ranks of the students. Democracy, however, is an abstract concept. Even more important, how is it to be put into practice and systematized? The students at Tienanmen apparently did not have any concrete plans for putting democracy into practice, but the idea of "democracy" clearly has already struck deep roots in the hearts of many people.

2. Communist China has strict clamps on freedom: Without democracy, there is no freedom naturally. Since the Chinese Communists seized power, they have proclaimed the dictatorship of the proletariat, but actually it is the dictatorship of the Communist Party. Common people do not even have the freedom to protect their lives or decide how to use their property, not to mention other freedoms or rights. The freedoms sought by the recent democracy movement were narrow in scope, with the main points being only freedom of speech and freedom of the press, but it is precisely against these two basic human rights that the Chinese Communists impose their strictest controls.

In order to consolidate their political power, the Chinese Communists have restricted the people's pursuit of knowledge. Their targets of oppression are especially intellectuals who think independently. Their method has been none other than to seal the voices and plug the ears of intellectuals. To silence the voices of the intellectuals, the Chinese Communist regime has in the past launched one political struggle after another: the Anti-rightist struggle in 1957 rounded up in one fell swoop all who dared to express their opinions; in 1966, the Gang of Four conducted a large-scale literary inquisition using the excuse that playwrights "used the past to disparage the present;" and in 1987, Fang Li-chih and others were transferred and suffered persecution for "polluting the thoughts of students." After enduring decades of Chinese Communist oppression, intellectuals in the Chinese mainland were driven beyond the limits of endurance and finally exploded in the recent pro-democracy movement, demanding freedom of speech.

In order to restrict what the people hear, the Communists control all mass media under the state and party. They dominate the appointment and removal of the media's personnel so as to control the direction and perspective of discourse. If certain media dare to speak the truth, they will be thoroughly eradicated. A most recent instance is Shanghai's *World Economic Report*. Disobeying the Communist Party's order, the paper reported the truth regarding the democracy movement in Tienanmen Square and was forced to reorganize, with the paper's editor-in-chief Chin Pen-li being removed. In short, the Communists have consistently rejected such concepts as the people's right to know, journalistic ethics, factual reporting, journalistic social responsibility, and public monitoring. They stubbornly insist that journalism serve politics, and that the news media should be a propaganda tool to promote socialism.

When mainland China was a closed society, almost totally isolated from the outside world, and all working opportunities were controlled by those in power, the majority of mainland people and journalists did not know about or dare to disagree with the way the Communists muzzled public opinion and controlled the mass media. As a result, the media in mainland China slowly became a big propaganda machine for the Communists' "Hall of One Voice." But as mainland China is forced to open its door to the world, and people learn more about the outside, their outlook broadens. As they realize they can live without the "Iron Rice Bowl," or a guaranteed job, they also begin to reflect on the difference between news and propaganda, and ask for the right to know, fair reporting, and public monitoring. During the democracy movement, even the reporters of the Communist official news agencies such as *New China News Agency* and the *People's Daily* joined the street demonstrations, and the staff of Hongkong's *Wen Wei Po* and *Ta Kung Pao* also criticized the Communists for persecuting the people, all of them risking loss of their jobs and being purged. It shows that people and journalists in the mainland clearly abhor the present situation where mass media are tightly controlled by the Communists.

3. The corruption of Chinese communist cadres: Since Teng Hsiao-ping took power ten years ago and proceeded to make economic reforms and adopt an open door policy, the economic situation in the mainland has indeed improved, and the living standards of the people are higher than before. Most of the gains of economic development, however, go to Chinese Communist Party cadres and their relatives. The veteran cadres who participated in the Long March, have the view that they should "sit and enjoy all from the domain they have won," and strive for material pleasures, indulgently wasting the fruits of the people's efforts. As for their children, grandchildren and sons-in-law, they are well taken care of by their elders. Some inherit their elders' positions and become high cadres involved in bribery and corruption, while others use their connections to engage in speculation and profiteering. Both of them share one common trait: they lead an extravagant life, a life apart from the common people, as far apart as heaven and earth. This situation prevails everywhere in the mainland, and though the people have noticed it, they dare only to be angry, not to speak, at most coining some satirical expressions to vent their spleen.

During the past two years, the economic situation on the mainland has worsened, due to over-investment and a growing trade deficit, which has led to inflation and soaring commodity prices. The lives of the common people are becoming harder day by day. In addition, given the inequitable distribution of wealth, individual owners and speculators become rich overnight, while the office employees, farmers and workers instead see their incomes reduced. Naturally, the people have become quite dissatisfied with the present situation.

Faced with a deteriorating economy, however, the Chinese Communists have never been able to offer effective measures in response, but only emphasize cutting consumption. They trumpet the slogan, "Break Through the Commodity Price Barrier," and ask the multitudes to "prepare for hard times." Yet the high cadres and their relatives continue abusing their privileges and leading lives of luxury, which unavoidably makes the people extremely angry. During the democracy movement, the crowds rallied most to the demands of "oppose corruption," "oppose abuse of privilege," and "disclose the property and income of party and government leaders and their children." Official corruption in Communist China clearly has become quite serious, and the people cannot tolerate it anymore.

4. Persecution of the intellectuals by the Chinese Communists: Intellectuals have the spirit that pursues new knowledge, the conscience that reflects and examines the self, the ability to think independently, and the habit of criticising the present situation. More im-

portantly, Chinese intellectuals have a traditional sense of responsibility to "take the world upon one's shoulders." All of these traits are potential threats to a dictatorship, because intellectuals can criticise, doubt, and even unmask lies, which could shake the foundations of the Chinese Communist regime. As a result, the Chinese Communists must do all in their power to suppress them.

Since seizing political power, the Chinese Communists have launched a series of campaigns to persecute intellectuals, starting with the Counter-revolutionary Elimination Movement in 1951, the Five Anti Movement in 1952, the Anti-rightist Movement in 1957, the Cultural Revolution and the Red Guards in 1966, and the movement to send down educated urban youth to work in the countryside and mountain areas in 1967. The intellectuals were disgraced as society's "stinking ninth class," the lowest of social strata.

When Teng took power, he had to rely on the professional knowledge of the intellectuals to carry out the Four Modernizations, and thus repression was slightly relaxed. The climate of discrimination against intellectuals, however, which has been fashioned purposefully over a long period, will not change in the short run. Living standards and working conditions for intellectuals have not improved to a reasonable extent. Consequently, such expressions as "Selling tea eggs beats studying atoms," and "Better barber's shears than a surgeon's scalpel," appear one after the other, revealing the intellectuals' resentment and sense of helplessness. Unwilling to further endure such humiliation, college students have raised their voices in recent years, demanding respect and reasonable treatment for intellectuals. The democracy movement is a full-scale explosion of the intellectuals' grievances. In addition to students, the people protesting in the streets included teachers, writers, scientific researchers, government workers, journalists, performing artists, and the intellectual elite that consults and makes plans for the Chinese Communists. The movement demonstrates that the discontent of the intellectuals has reached its limit, and that they will not take it any more.

Problems appear one after another in mainland China, and they all basically stem from the Chinese Communists holding the political reins without regard to global trends or the people's interests. The four problems above became so pressing as to require an immediate solution, which brought about an explosion of popular emotion and action, and was the main cause of the large-scale popular movement and the consequent massacre. Other factors which functioned as catalysts were:

a. The Open Door Policy: The Chinese Communists in the past few years have adopted an open door policy in some areas, hoping to revive the mainland's economy. Foreign capital, businesses, and technology have made their way into mainland China and assisted its economic development considerably. In the meantime, however, such modernizing concepts as democracy, freedom, and the rule of law have also steadily seeped into the mainland. In addition, basic operating principles of modern economics, such as fair competition and more pay for more work, have also been introduced in a major way. These have all had a great impact on the previously closed society of mainland China, leading the people to reflect and examine their own situation. They now seek to catch up with the rest of the world.

b. The Taiwan Experience: Recently, the government of the Republic of China has allowed Taiwan residents to visit their relatives on the mainland, and accepted applications from mainlanders to visit sick relatives in the ROC or attend their funerals, and for visits to the ROC by eminent mainlanders. In addition, mail and telecommunications links between Taiwan and the mainland are allowed. As a result, people living on either side of the Taiwan Straits have gotten a glimpse of life on the other side. The economic prosperity and constitutional democracy of Taiwan have made people on the mainland sit up and think. Given the similarities in language, ethnic, and cultural background, the inspiration and impact of the "Taiwan experience" on the mainland should be even stronger than that of "American or Japanese experience."

c. The Rise Of Individual Owners: After the Communists began their limited opening of the economy, they allowed private individuals to run small businesses, who became known as the "individual owners." Successful individual owners are similar to the middle classes of the West, and generally scholars acknowledge that the formation of a middle class can facilitate political democratization.

d. Technological Advancement: The advancement of technology, espcially in transportation and communications, is closely related to democratic freedom. Devious means designed to keep the people in ignorance, such as monopolizing the flow of information, news blackouts, and fabricating rumors are gradually losing their place, and the environment that allowed dictators behind the Bamboo and Iron Curtains to do what they liked can no longer be maintained.

III. An Intense and Sharp Response

This sort of massive movement for democracy and freedom and accompanying ruthless suppression naturally received the world's attention. The movement won world support from the beginning, and after the bloody suppression of June 4, support activities reached a climax. Severe condemnation and sanctions against the Chinese Communist regime came from all corners of the world, with those from the Taiwan-Pescadores region of Free China being especially ardent.

In order not to give the Chinese Communist authorities an excuse for the crackdown, our government at first did not react strongly to the democracy movement. It was not until May 20 when Yang Shang-kun ordered a military push into Peking, Li Peng imposed martial law, and the Chinese Communist authorities ordered a news blackout, that official concern for the demonstration was voiced by ROC government spokesman Shaw Yu-ming, who sternly warned the Chinese Communist authorities "to stop at once the use of military force in suppressing the people's movement, to restore the rights of Chinese and foreign journalists to report the truth, and to abandon all its tyrannical measures." Consequently, the Executive Yuan's ad hoc Task Force on Mainland Affairs proclaimed its support for the democracy movement on the mainland, and Premier Yu Kuo-hwa voiced our concerns in a speech. After the massacre on June 4, President Lee Teng-hui, attending the Second Plenary Session of the 13th Central Committee of the Kuomintang at Yangmingshan, made a statement on behalf of the ROC government regarding the bloody crackdown of the student movement by the Chinese Communists. In it, he solemnly summoned all peace-loving nations and peoples of the world who share a concern for human rights to sternly condemn the Chinese Communists, to demand an immediate stop to the bloody massacre, and to offer the best of care and relief to the wounded and families of the dead.

President Lee also called on all Chinese people at home and abroad to show their great love for their countrymen, to unite behind their mainland compatriots in their struggle for survival and freedom, to support and assist them in every possible way, and to sever all ties with the Chinese Communists. In another statement on behalf of the ROC government, Shaw Yu-ming, Director-General of the Government Information Office, condemned the violent acts of the Chinese Communists. In the days that followed, President Lee Teng-hui, the newly appointed Premier Lee Huan and many other senior officials of our government continued to express the ROC government's position.

The Legislative Yuan along with other representative bodies offered their support on behalf of the people of Taiwan. The Cabinet-level ad hoc Committee on Mainland Affairs also passed an "Action Program for Supporting the Democracy Movement in the Mainland." The ruling party, the Kuomintang, likewise expressed its deep concern for the movement. As early as May 17, KMT chairman Lee Teng-hui expressed his sympathy and support for the democracy movement on the mainland in a speech to the party's Central Standing Committee. On the same day, the KMT Central Committee issued a solemn statement. On May 24, at the KMT Central Standing Committee meeting Chairman Lee again asked all concerned offices to take effective measures as soon as possible to support the students' movement, lest their blood and tears should be shed in vain and their enthusiasm wasted. On June 7, Chairman Lee again directed the government to use tranquillity to master the dynamic in order to assist mainland Chinese realize democracy. Later he continued to express his opinion about this matter many times. James C.Y. Soong, Secretary-General of the KMT Central Committee, also expressed deep concern about the matter on behalf of the ruling party.

Opposition parties also unanimously expressed their extreme disgust at the acts of violence by the Chinese Communists and showed their support of the democracy movement in a variety of ways.

During these hours of sorrow, civic organizations and people of all walks of life took action in enthusiastic support. They contributed money, donated blood, gave materials, and offered their wisdom and labor. Everyone devoted their efforts to the support movement, and large-scale support activities continued throughout Taiwan.

—On May 23, students and teachers from 21 colleges issued separate statements supporting the democracy movement on the mainland. Many other schools held petition drives, made Statues of Liberty, and held rallies.

—At 12:30 on May 31, around 100,000 students and youths took part in an islandwide rally dubbed "Hand in Hand, Heart to Heart." The participants joined hands along Taiwan's North-South Provincial Highway, with the line of people stretching from the northern port city of Keelung to the southern port of Kaohsiung. Hualien, Ilan, Taitung, and Penghu counties also held similar rallies.

—Rallies of over 10,000 people initiated by civic organizations, entertainers, and journalists were continuously held at Taipei's Chiang Kai-shek Memorial Hall and Sun Yat-sen Memorial Hall.

Similar rallies could also be seen in large public places in central and southern Taiwan. A song, "The Wound of History," was taped and played everywhere.

—Three television stations and many radio stations rearranged their programming and aired news about the democracy movement on the mainland and rallies of support around Taiwan. Newspapers also published extensive reports about the movement.

—Literary figures held meetings, poetry recitations, wrote poems and created paintings to express their support.

—Businessmen held many activities of support, and some advertised their support in newspapers.

—In an open letter, the Grand Alliance for Reunification of China Under the Three Principles of the People proclaimed its condemnation of the atrocities of the Chinese Communist regime. The Grand Alliance has also passed the "Emergency Measures to Support the Democratic Movement on the Mainland," to give active support.

—On June 8, religious leaders expressed their indignation by ringing bells, fasting and praying, raising money, and conducting petition drives.

The ardent support in Taiwan was echoed by overseas Chinese students abroad everywhere, whether from Taiwan, the mainland, Hongkong, or Macao, as all joined in support. Reactions in Hongkong and Macao were especially furious, due in part to fears over the transfer of Hongkong to China in 1997.

Many nations declared sanctions against the Chinese Communist regime, with the United States, Western European countries, Japan, and countries of Oceania and Southeast Asia unanimously condemning the massacre. Australian Prime Minister Robert Hawke sobbed and wept as he denounced the killing. Even such traditionally neutral states such as Switzerland, Austria, Sweden, and Finland decided to freeze economic relations with Peking.

In France, one of the earlier countries to establish diplomatic relations with the Chinese Communists, President François Mitterand declared a freezing of all bilateral relations. The twelve member nations of the European Community halted contacts with Peking, and discussed possible economic sanctions on June 26. A meeting between a delegation led by the Minister of Foreign Economic Relations and Trade Cheng To-pin and the European Community committee in Brussels was canceled. In addition, the U.S. visit by the Chinese Communist foreign minister Chien Chi-chen was cut short.

The United States government, moreoever, has announced it will discontinue military exchange programs with the Chinese Communists, and the World Bank has decided to suspend loans to mainland China. Both are substantial blows to the Chinese Communists.

IV. Effects of the Democracy Movement

The world rarely sees a movement of the duration, scale and loss of life comparable to that of the recent democracy movement in mainland China. The movement will have serious effects on the Chinese Communist regime, with the following changes being worthy of our attention:

1. The authority of the Chinese Communists has been damaged: The Chinese people on the mainland from the start did not evince any support for the way the Communist authorities handled the democracy movement and ignored the martial law regulations, even resorting to revolutionary methods and using their bodies and rocks to fight Chinese Communist soldiers. Their actions have already seriously damaged the ruling authority of the Chinese Communists. In order to rebuild their authority, the Chinese Communists will intensify their suppression and continue mass arrests and the rectification movement for some time.

2. The ruling class will tend to become more conservative: Various factions within the Chinese Communist ruling class held different views on handling the democracy movement. The hardline conservative faction clearly won, and the power of the moderates will be greatly reduced. The political and economic policies of the Chinese Communist regime will tend to become more conservative.

3. The power of the military will be strengthened even further: The Chinese Communists used the military to carry out the massacre and suppress the democracy movement by force, proving again that their true nature is "political power comes out of the barrel of the gun." To maintain their power, Teng Hsiao-ping and his cohorts must rely even more on the military. Moreover, the position of the Chinese Communist military leaders has become even firmer, and they may seek even more power.

4. Intellectuals will be persecuted again: The democracy movement, initiated by intellectuals and carried out by students, infuriat-

ed the Chinese Communists. This anger will be directed again at the intellectuals, and a massive rectification movement is unavoidable. The Chinese Communists, however, may improve working conditions for intellectuals in order to pacify them, but will also place them under stricter supervision to prevent another large scale democracy movement.

5. Control of the news media will be tightened: During the democracy movement, the Chinese Communists believed that the statements and actions of many in the media were tantamount to rebellion, which not only made the Chinese Communists lose face but also deepened their crisis mentality. Therefore the Chinese Communists will surely reorganize the news media to strengthen their control over public opinion.

6. Possible agitation of anti-foreign sentiment: The Chinese Communists have a tendency to blame foreign powers, with the intention of encouraging nationalism by inciting anti-foreign sentiments, and thus shift attention away from their own blunders. The activities of the foreign news media and members of the Taiwan and Hongkong press will be severely limited, and diplomatic feuds with various countries will increase.

The six trends described above may all develop within a short time. In the long run, however, because these developments run counter to the will of the people in mainland China, a regime which has committed so much injustice will come to no good end, even though the Chinese Communists have been able to temporarily suppress the democracy movement on the Chinese mainland through severe repression and terror. It can be seen already through the anti-Communist actions by the mainland Chinese and the numerous defections by mainland students and diplomatic personnel abroad.

One of the leaders of mainland China democracy movement, Yen Chia-chi, concluded in a letter he wrote when he fled to Hongkong: "Teng Hsiao-ping has sowed the seeds of a storm of hatred. Government by terror and policies of extinction will never bring Teng Hsiao-ping, Li Peng, Yang Shang-kun and the reactionary cliques many years of peace and quiet. They have sowed the seeds of the storm of hatred, and in the not-too-distant future, they will reap an awesome hurricane that will engulf all of China. They will be severely judged by the people, and the dictatorial empire of Teng Hsiao-ping on which their survival depends will disintegrate in an instant." As Yen Chia-chi said, the democracy movement on mainland China has already rung the death knell for the despotic regime of the Chinese Communists. As a result, we believe that all Chinese will do all in their power to hasten the fall of the Chinese Communist regime.

A Statement by the Government of the Republic of China, on the Movement for Freedom and Democracy in Mainland China

(May 21, 1989)

The Chinese Communist regime announced that starting from 10 a.m. yesterday (May 20), martial law would be imposed on Peking, and troops would be dispatched to suppress students and other social classes participating in the movement for freedom and democracy. At the same time, a news blackout was imposed, and both Chinese and foreign journalists engaged in newsgathering activities were prohibited from reporting, taking photographs and maintaining contact with the outside world. We are deeply pained and condemn the Chinese Communists authorities for depriving the people of their freedom of assembly, demonstration, speech, and press, and for totally ignoring Chinese and foreign opinions.

This surging movement for freedom and democracy by our several-million mainland compatriots that include students, workers, journalists, civil servants, army and police, fully shows that the Chinese Communist regime has misruled the mainland for the last four decades and has thus been abandoned unanimously by the Chinese people on the mainland. Instead of reflecting on and correcting their misrule, the Chinese Communist leaders are using military force to suppress movements initiated by the masses, which fully exposes the Chinese Communist tyranny and its barbarian nature.

Our government and the people, with deep concern, are all closely watching the developments of the turmoil on the mainland, and are deliberating effective measures in response to it. Today, the people and government of the Republic of China formally proclaim to our mainland compatriots that we vow to act as the rear guard in their movement for freedom and democracy and that we will join hands with them to fight unremittingly for a bright future for China. At the same time we would like to sternly warn the Chinese Communist regime to stop at once the use of military force in suppressing people's movements, to restore Chinese and foreign journalists' rights to report, to1abandon all its tyrannical measures, and to march toward the goal of political democratization, economic liberalization, social pluralism, and the renaissance of Chinese culture.

Statement on the Situation in Mainland China

LEE Teng-hui
President
Republic of China
June 4, 1989

Ladies and Gentlemen:

Early this morning, Chinese Communist troops finally used military force to attack the students and others demonstrating peacefully for democracy and freedom in Tienanmen Square in Peking, resulting in heavy casualties and loss of life. Although we anticipated this mad action of the Chinese Communists beforehand, it still has moved us to incomparable grief, indignation, and shock.

We believe that the existence of any political power must be based on the will of the people. The Chinese Communists were able to usurp the Chinese mainland with violence and lies, but there have been constant internal struggles and suppression of the people over the past forty years. In the face of a universal awakening of our mainland countrymen, the inhumane actions of the Chinese Communists are sure to be judged by history, evoke even stronger opposition from our mainland countrymen, and hasten the demise of the Chinese Communists.

With a deeply grieved and heavy heart, I wish, on behalf of the government and people of the Republic of China, to summon all the peace-loving nations and people of the world who share a concern for human rights to sternly condemn the Chinese Communists; to demand them to put an immediate stop to this bloody massacre; and to demand them to offer their best care and relief to the wounded and families of the dead.

I also summon all Chinese people at home and abroad to put their great love for their countrymen into practice, to closely unite and act as a backup for our mainland compatriots in their struggle for survival and freedom, to support and assist them in every way possible, and to make a complete break with the Chinese Communists.

At the same time, I also wish to remind the people on our bastion of national revival, military and civilian alike, to remain alert to the

Chinese Communists' inclination towards the use of violence and military force, and to be prepared, on the eve of the collapse of the Chinese Communists, for any action that they might risk taking.

The Chinese Communist tyranny is the shame of all the Chinese people of the world. The government and people of the Republic of China must resolutely unite all anti-communist and patriotic forces and exert their utmost efforts to overthrow this tyranny. We pledge not to stop until we have achieved this goal.

Press Release of the Government Information Office, Executive Yuan

June 4, 1989

At 5 P.M. on 4 June 1989, Dr. Shaw Yu-ming, director-general of the Government Information Office, Executive Yuan, issued the following statement on the suppression of the democracy movement by the Chinese Communists to foreign journalists posted in the Republic of China.

1) The armed suppression of the democracy movement reveals the barbarity, savagery, and near madness of the Chinese Communists. It is a tragic example in modern history of the massacre of one's own countrymen. Someone on the mainland pointed out that this action has caused more resentment than the great slaughter in Nanking by the Japanese in 1937. The 4th of June 1989 will stand as the darkest day in the Chinese Communists' rule of the mainland.

2) This action by the Chinese Communists has already deprived them of their legitimacy to rule, and caused Chinese at home and abroad as well as people throughout the world to condemn them. The Chinese Communists can never again claim to represent the Chinese people and rule the mainland.

3) This year marks the 70th anniversary of the May 4th Movement, the 40th anniversary of the establishment of the illegitimate government of the Chinese Communists, and the 200th anniversary of the French Revolution. Because of this, to the people who are striving for freedom and democracy on the mainland, this year can be said to have great historical significance and serve to encourage them.

4) Dealing in this way with unarmed crowds conducting peaceful demonstrations will surely provoke the hatred of the people, and in the future students and the general population will certainly carry out a prolonged struggle with the Chinese Communists, including armed revolution.

5) During the past month, Chinese all over the world have condemned the Chinese Communists with one voice, setting off a tide to unanimously cast aside the Chinese Communist regime. This type of situation in which there is a total consensus among Chinese

at home and abroad was seen only during the latter years of the Ching dynasty (A.D. 1644-1911). This has profound historical significance.

6) Even though some people believe that this student movement is only a struggle within the system, and not a revolutionary movement directed against the Chinese Communists from outside the system, we must point out that in spite of the fact that demonstrating crowds have not unanimously called for the overthrow of the Chinese Communists, they have absolutely not voiced support for them either. Looking deeper, we can discover that their slogan "democracy or death" and the shaping and erecting of a statue of the "Goddess of Liberty" in Tienanmen Square in every way prove that they are fighting for western style democracy. They do not dare to directly advocate the overthrow of the Chinese Communist regime because they want to avoid being branded "counter-revolutionaries" and being sentenced and thrown into prison.

7) In the future, our government and people will carry out the following actions:

—Continue the policy of opening up to the mainland and propagating the Taiwan experience. People who go to the mainland to visit relatives, attend meetings, gather news, and shoot films are catalysts in the movement toward democratization on the mainland. Because of this, people to people contacts should not stop.

—Public contributions and other forms of relief will be sent via the Red Cross organization in our country to support the people of the mainland.

—The Army, Navy, and Air Force will be put on full alert to guard against all contingencies.

—We call on the governments and people of countries throughout the world to condemn this outrage, to halt military and economic aid and sales to the Chinese Communists, and to stop transfers of high technology.

—We call on the international press corps to expand coverage of the real situation on the mainland to the whole world so as to expose the despotic government of the mainland and to convey the support of our government and people for the democratic movement on the mainland. Also, the Chinese Communists have used violence against reporters, and this must be sternly condemned by the international press corps.

Statement by the ROC Government In Regard to the Continued Killings by the Chinese Communists of Supporters of the Democracy Movement In Mainland China

June 22, 1989

1. Reliable sources have informed us that the Chinese Communist regime, since resorting to bloody, military force on June 4 to suppress the democracy movement on the mainland, have now unleashed a reign of terror to arrest participants and supporters of the movement. We are informed that more than 1,000 arrests have been made to date. This continued horror has resulted in a wave of shock and indignation that has swept around the world. The Chinese Communist regime has now become a public enemy to the whole world and has been discreited by all Chinese people and people of all countries who value democracy, freedom and justice.

2. Yesterday (June 21), the Chinese Communist regime killed three members of the democracy movement in public executions in Shanghai. According to the report, some of those under arrest in Peking will suffer the same tragic fate. This inhuman action again demonstrates the brutality and cruelty of the Chinese Communist regime, and has brought vehement condemnation from civilized nations all over the world. Some nations have one-by-one imposed sanctions against the Peking regime in hope of stopping the carnage.

3. On the occasion of the bloody massacre in the Chinese mainland, the government of the Republic of China solemnly states its position as follows:

a. To all the participants in the pro-democracy movement, our countrymen, and the anti-Communist overseas Chinese: The people and government of the Republic of China will stand by you forever. From now on, we will be unstinting in fighting for democracy and freedom for all Chinese until the Chinese Communist tyrannical government perishes from the Chinese mainland.

b. To all the countries, international organizations and people throughout the world that love democracy, freedom, and justice:

We deeply admire your opinions and actions taken in support of the pro-democracy movement in the mainland; the human concern and love shared by all manknind have been given full play once again. In view of the continued cruelty and suppression by the Chinese Communists, we call for your long-term rejection of and sanctions against the Chinese Communist government in the interest of humanity and justice — for which the Chinese Communist government has shown no respect or compassion through their actions, nor any repentance in the wake of their bloody deeds.

Illustrations

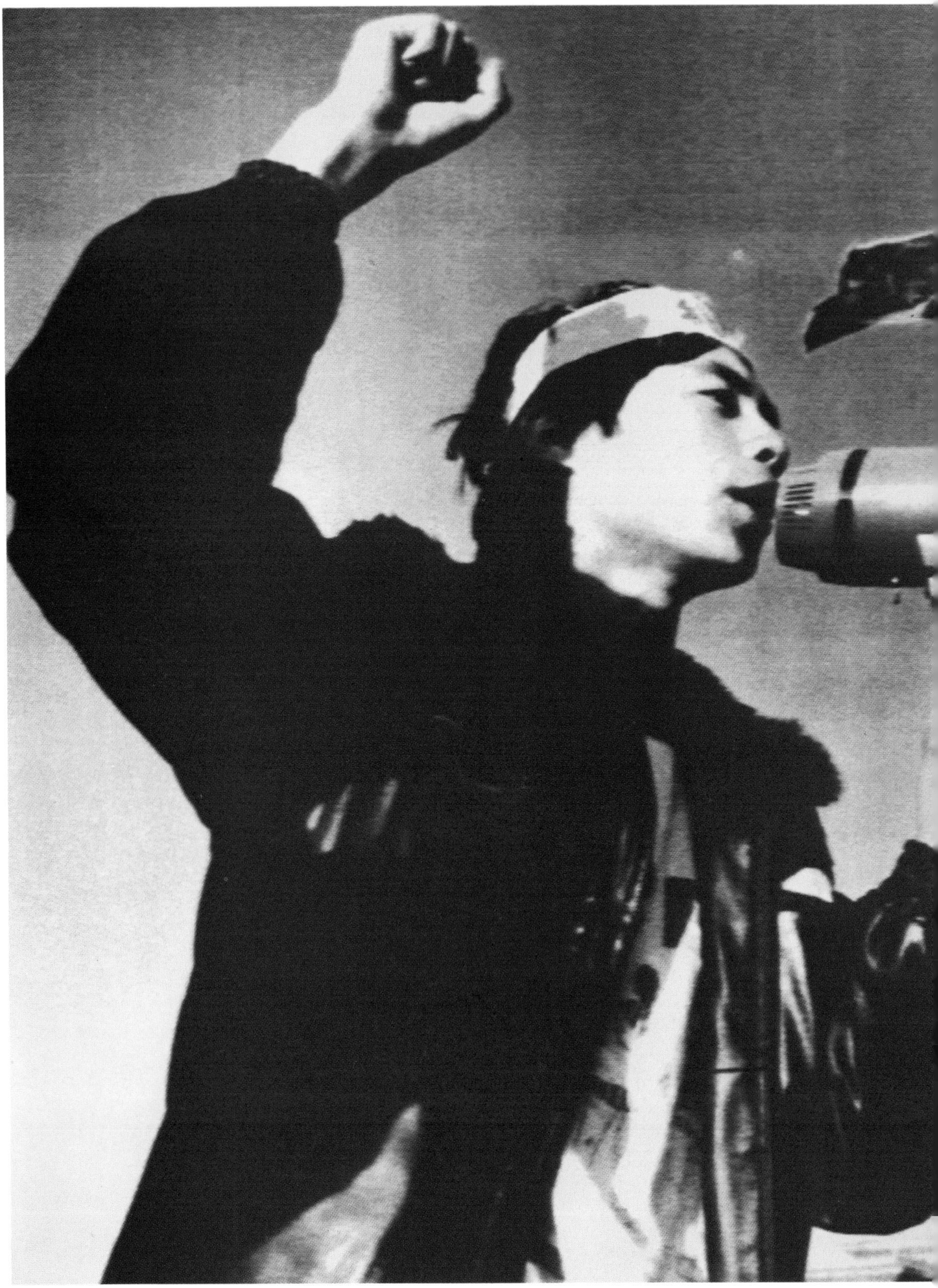

The Cry for Democracy

Student leader Wang Tan raises fist, voice for freedom. (AP)

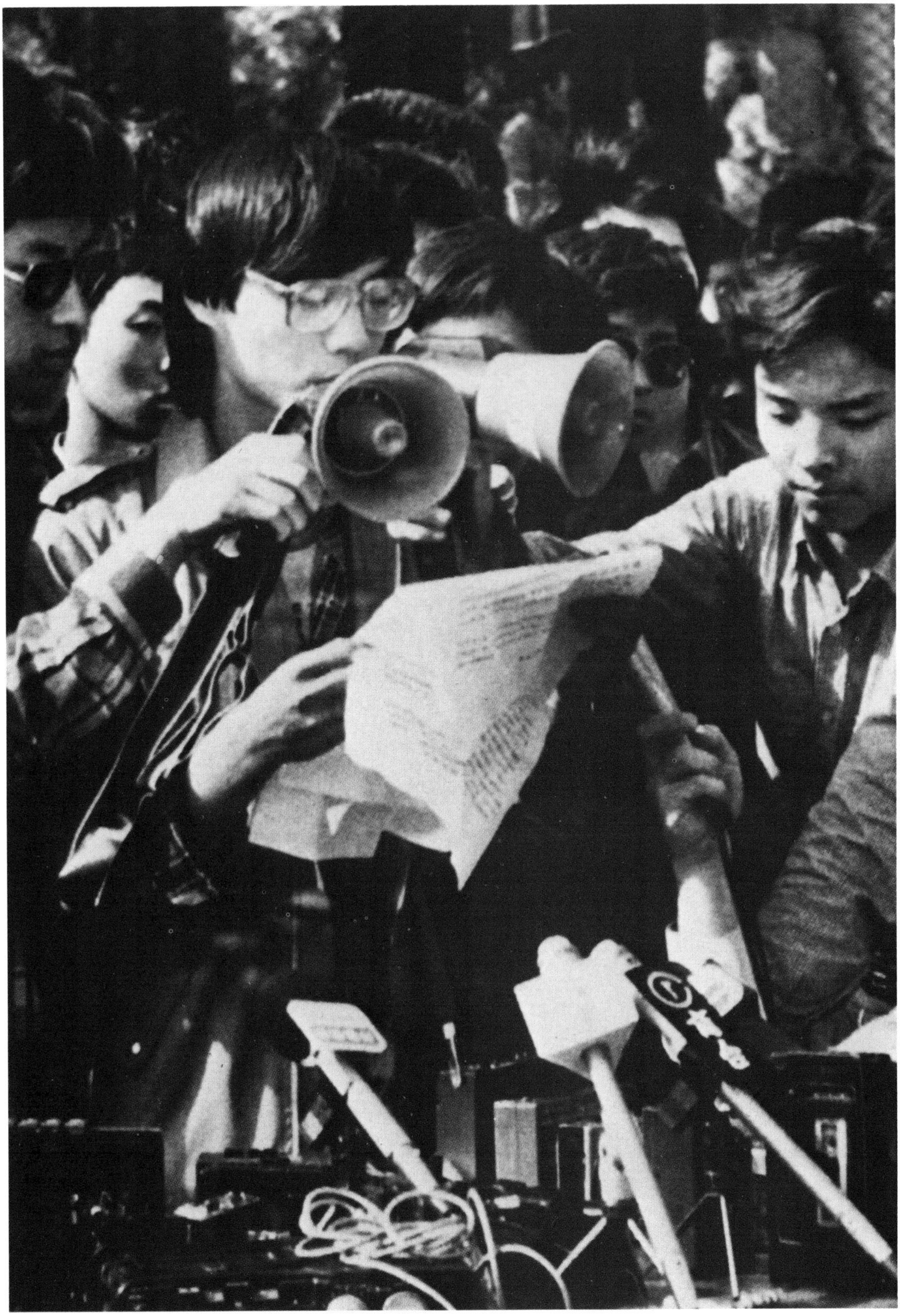

1. Wu'er Kai-hsi rebels at "black sun" darkening mainland. (AP)
2. Students mourn, march when Hu Yao-pang died. (AP)
3. Wang Tan decries Peking hypocrisy, May 1, Tienamen. (Reuters)

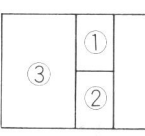

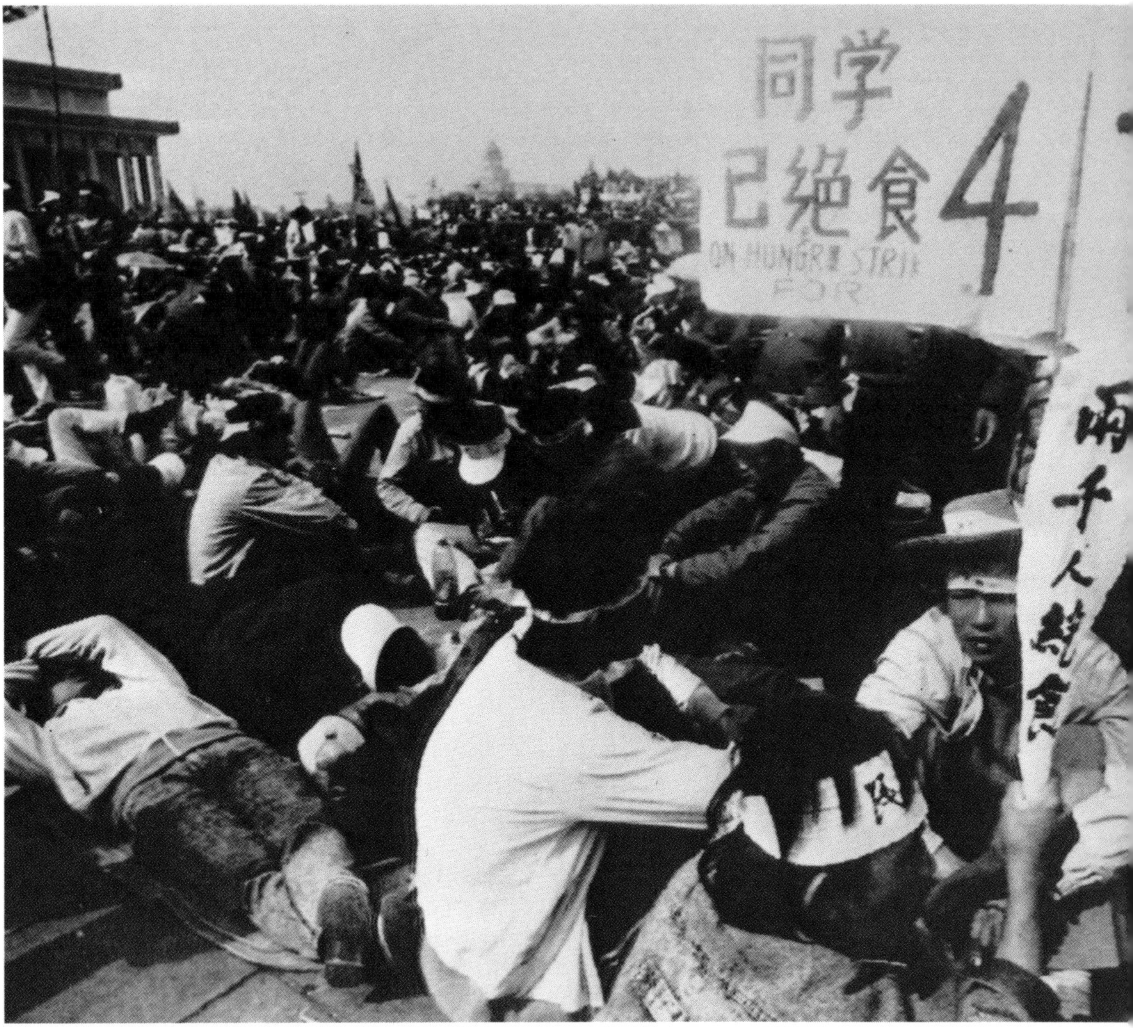
同学
已絶食 4
兩千人絶食

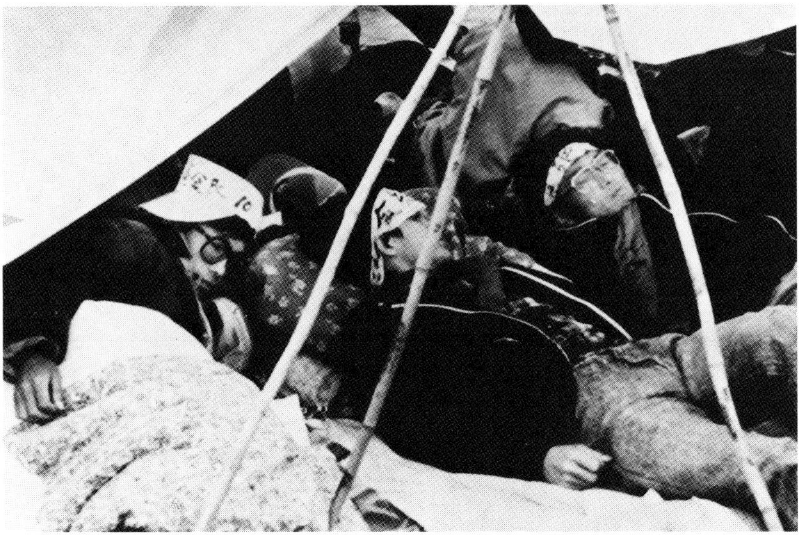

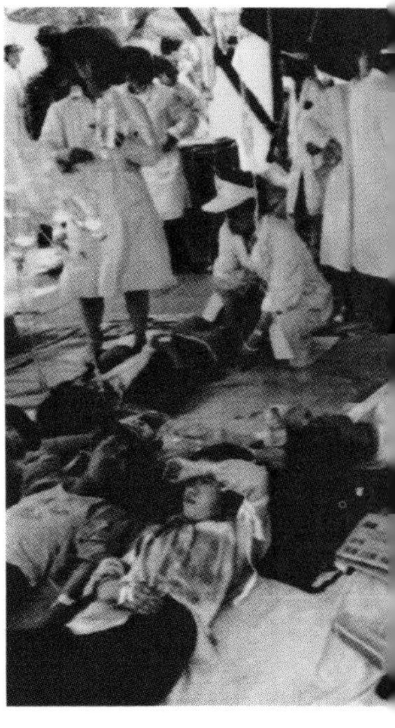

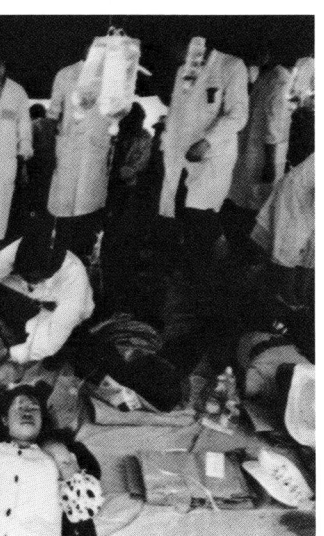

1. Party boss Chao Tzu-yang implores students to break fast. (AP)
2. Student hunger-strikers, 47th hour of fast. (Pao Cheng-ping)
3. Medics treat famished demonstrators. (AP)
4. Students fight hunger in Tienamen tent. (AP)

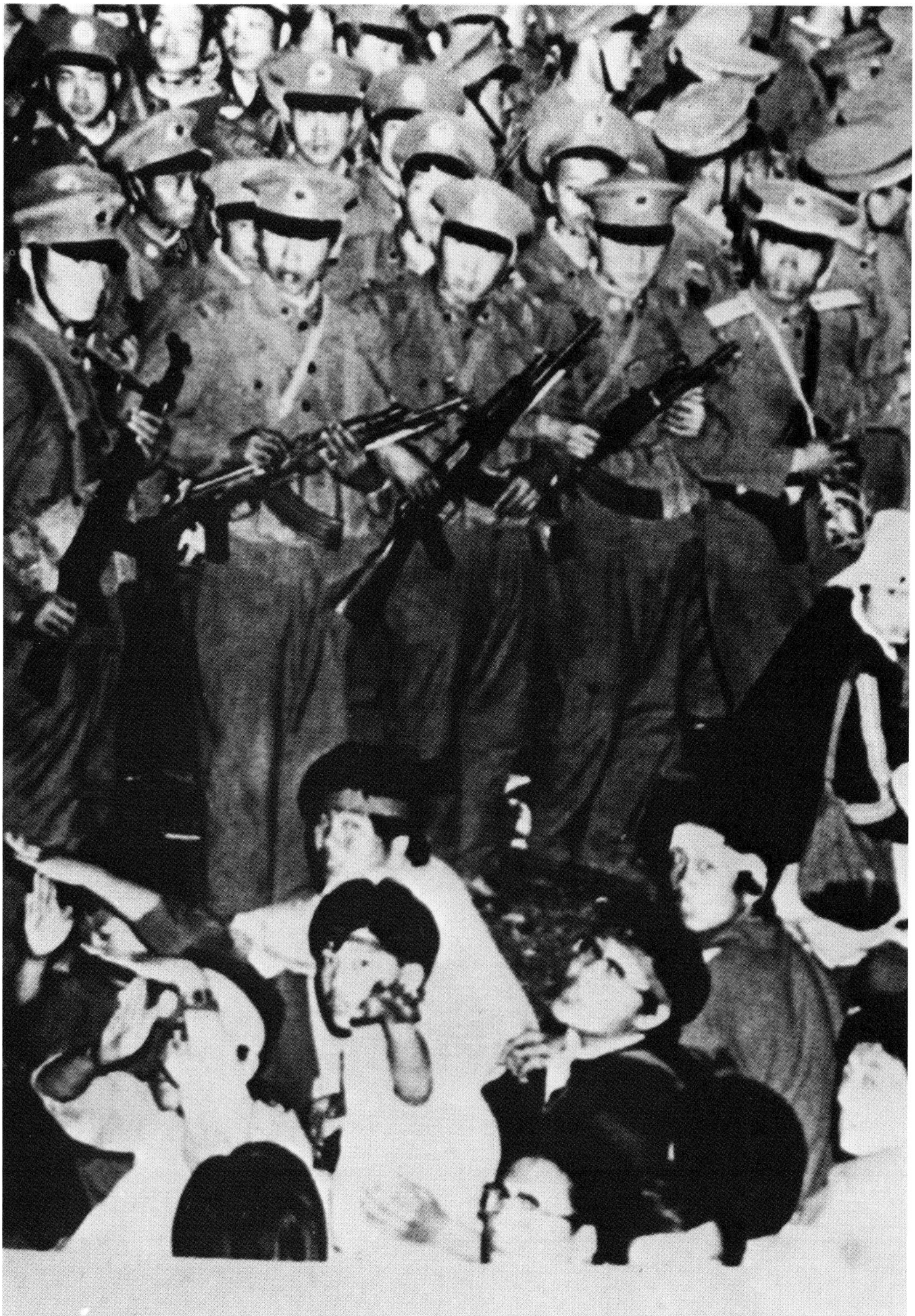

1. Student screams in fury and frustration. (AP)
2. Flesh-vs-armor; youths block army vehicle on airport road. (AP)
3. Woman joins protest; shouts: "Down with Li Peng!" (Reuters)
4. Unarmed students sit in path of troops marching on Peking. (AP)

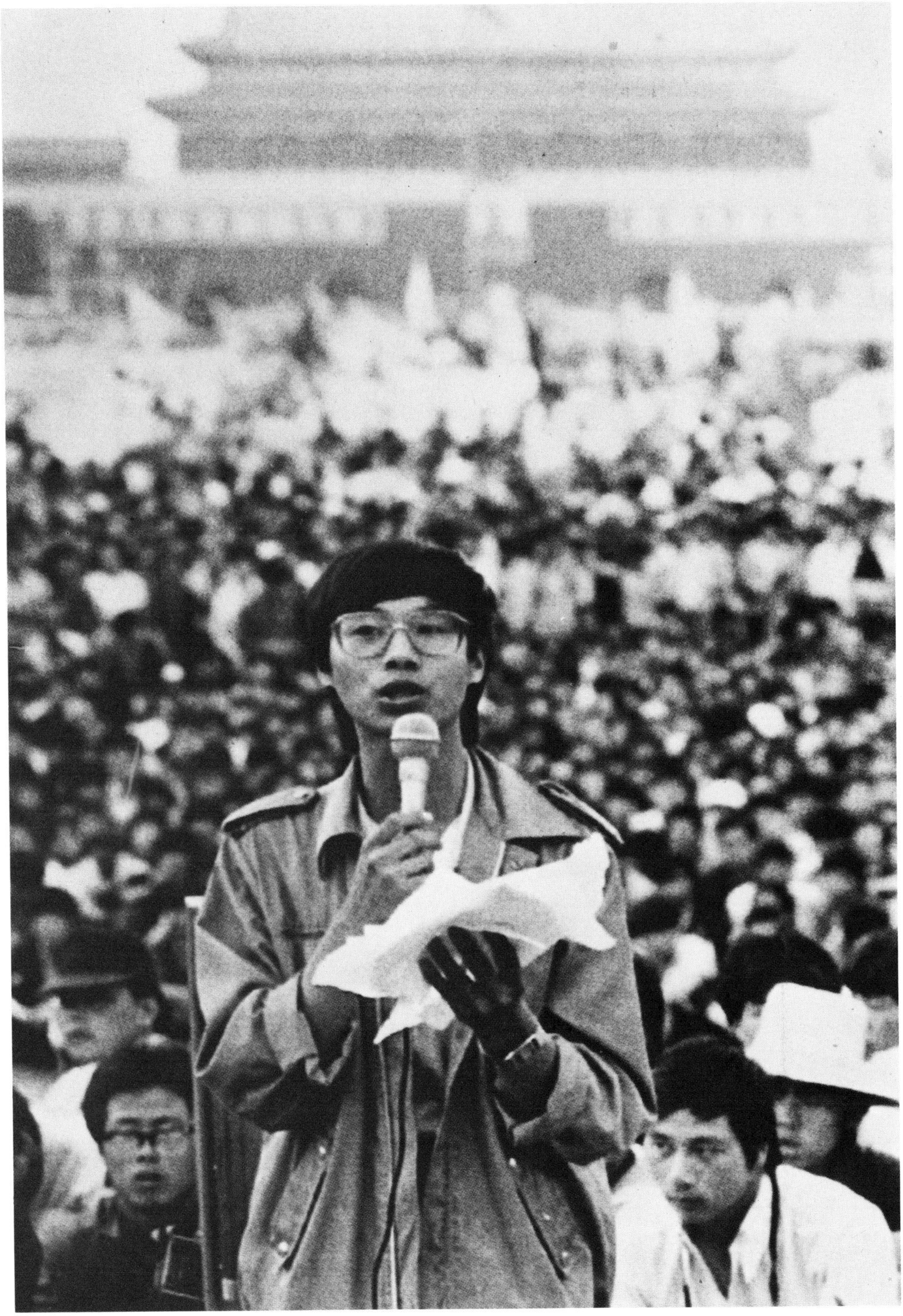

1. Students leave; a baby dreams in Tienamen Square, May 29. (AP)
2. Give up movement? Go back to school? Students debate. (Reuters)
3. May 27: Student leader Wang Tan orders Tienamen evacuated. (AP)

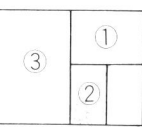

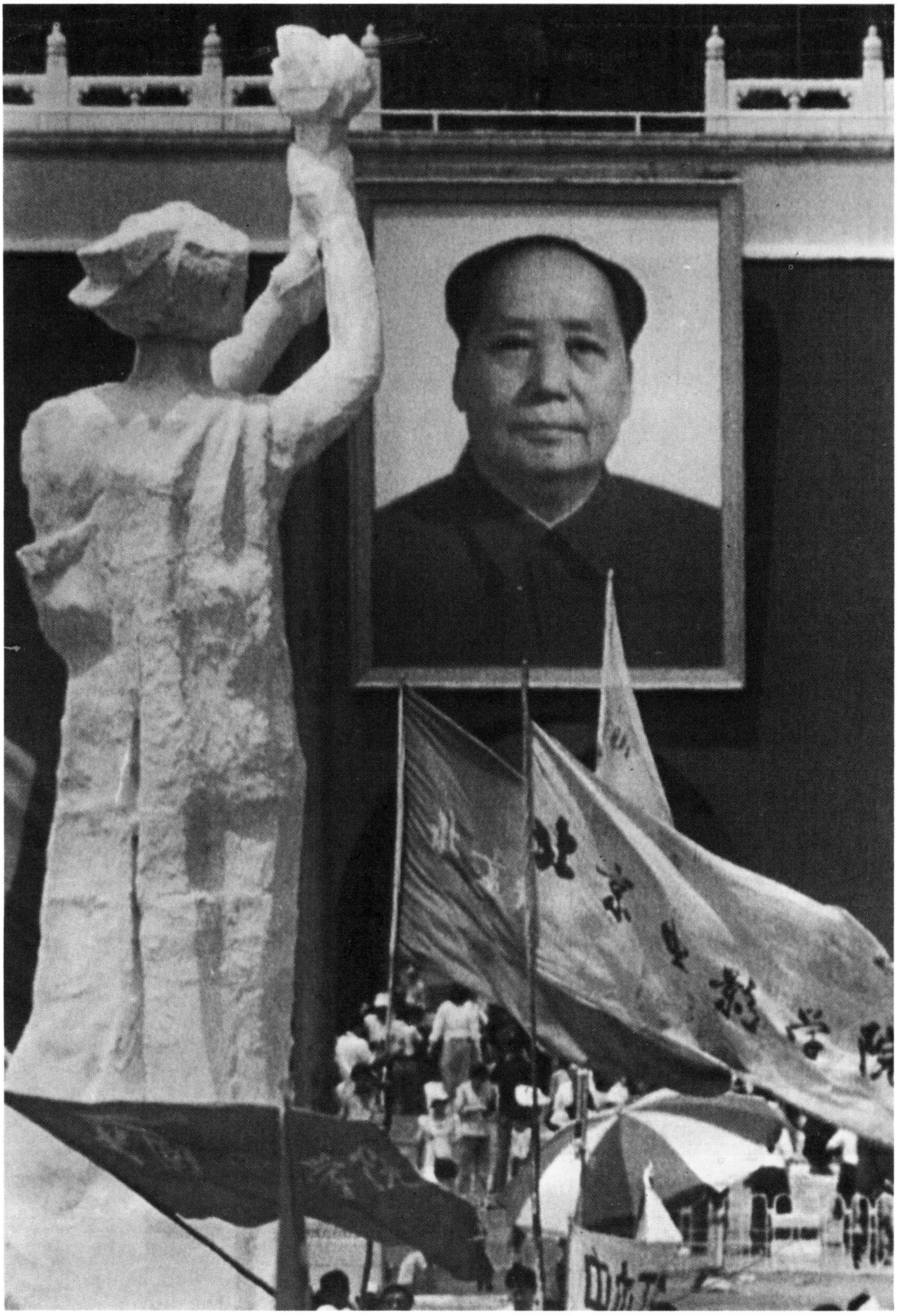

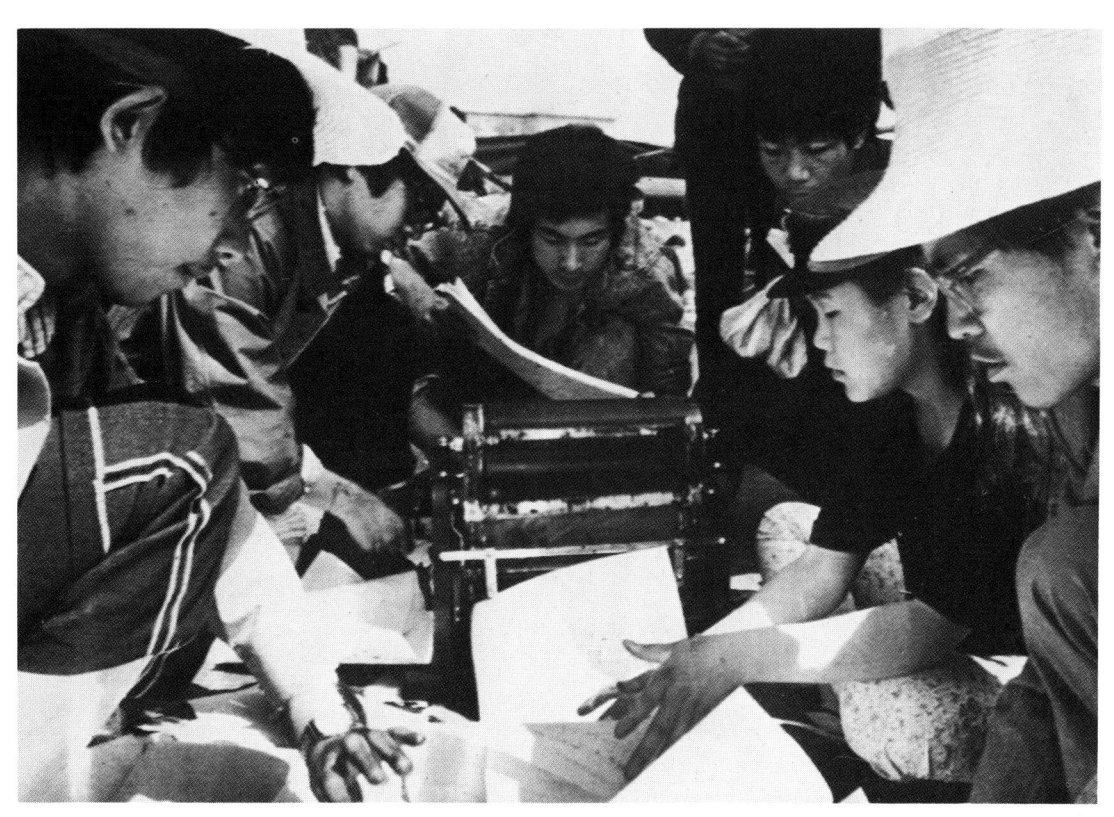

1. Free press: Students mimeo pro-democracy leaflets. (Reuters)
2. May 30: "Goddess of Democracy" raised; confronts Mao. (Reuters)

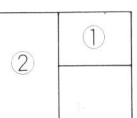

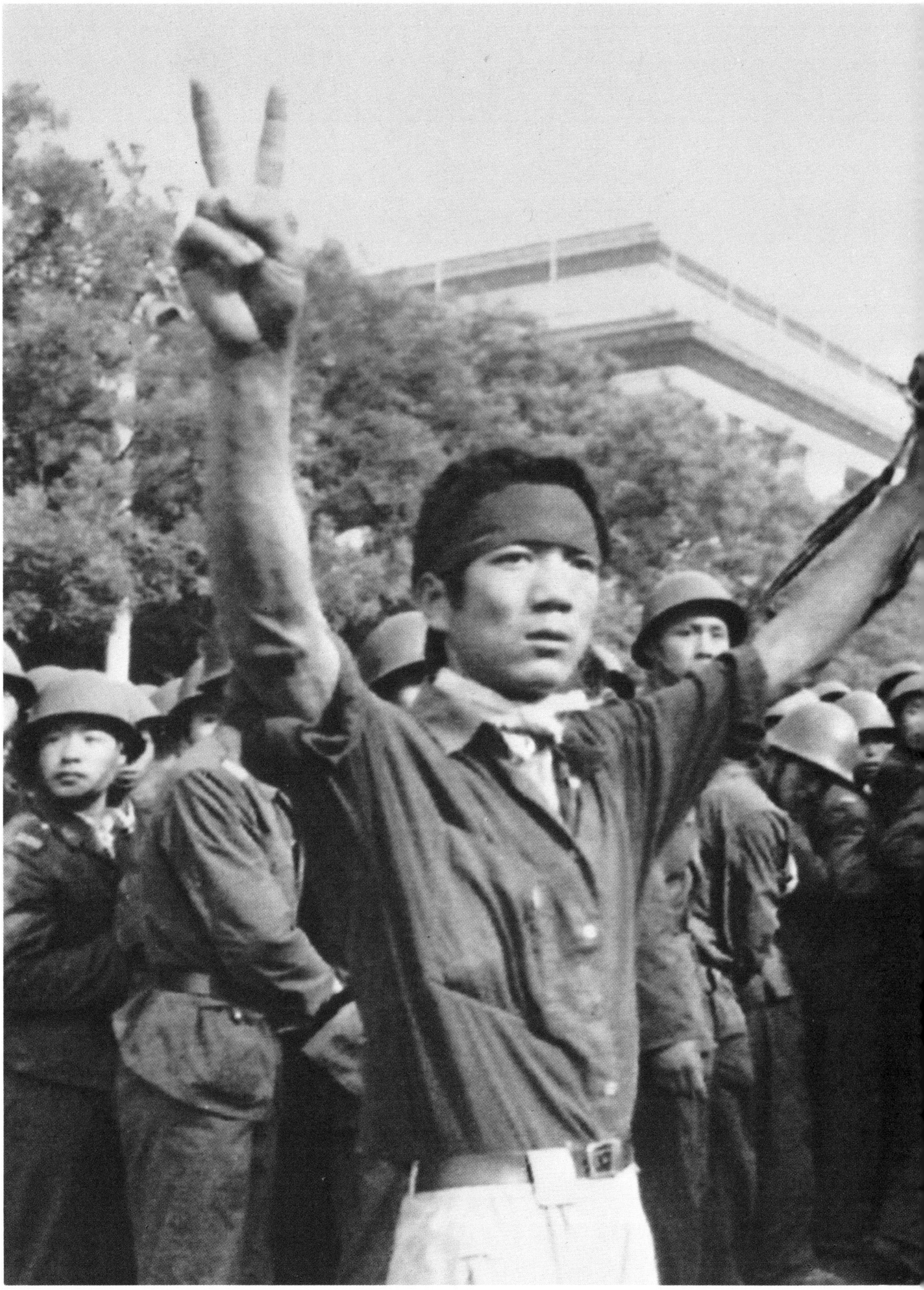

1. Singer stirs Tienamen with freedom road songs. (Reuters)
2. Grim-visaged student gives "Victory" sign as troops leave. (AP)

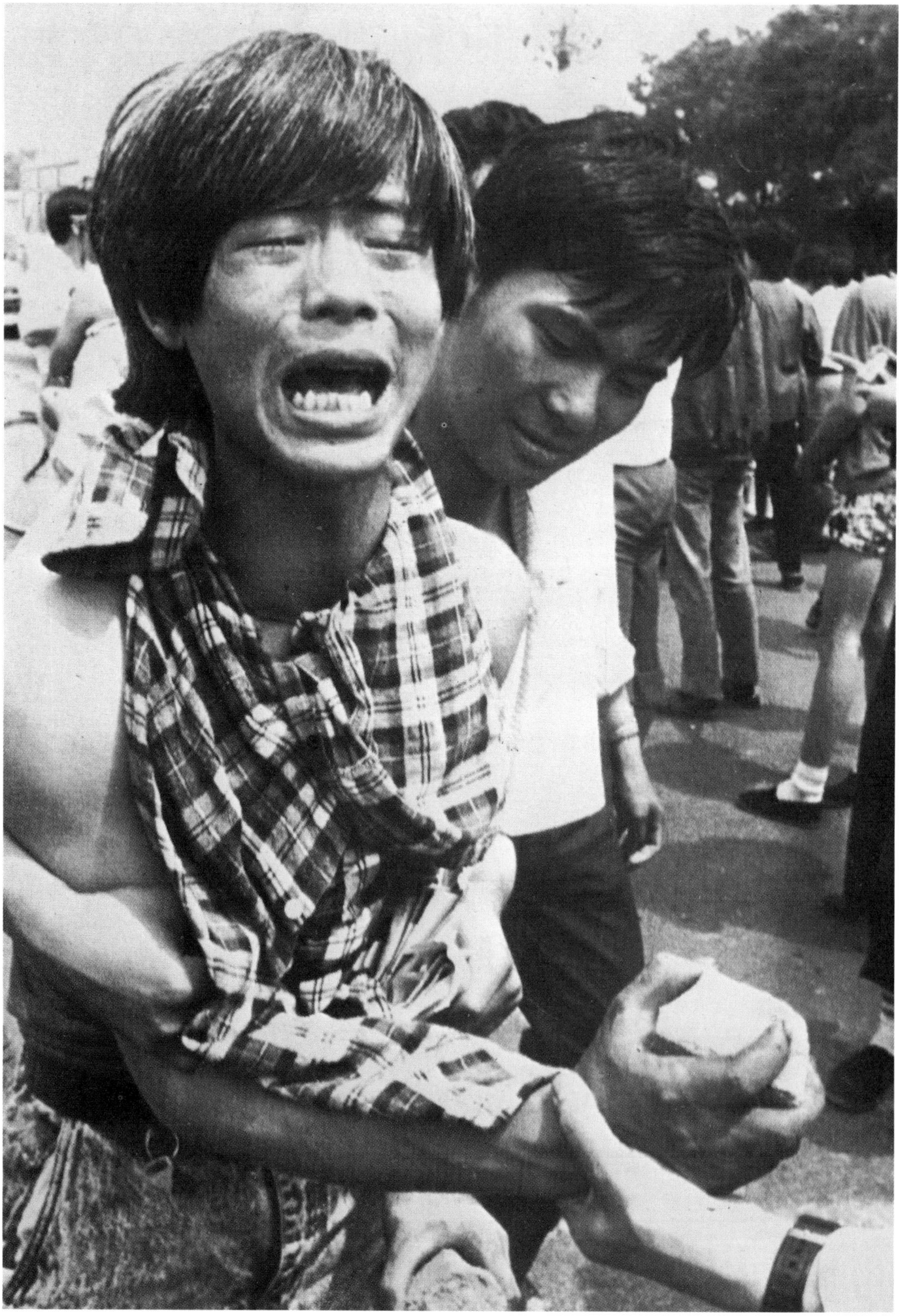

1. Singer Hou Teh-chien fasts at "Heroes" monument. (Reuters)
2. Tearful student is restrained from stoning troops. (Reuters)

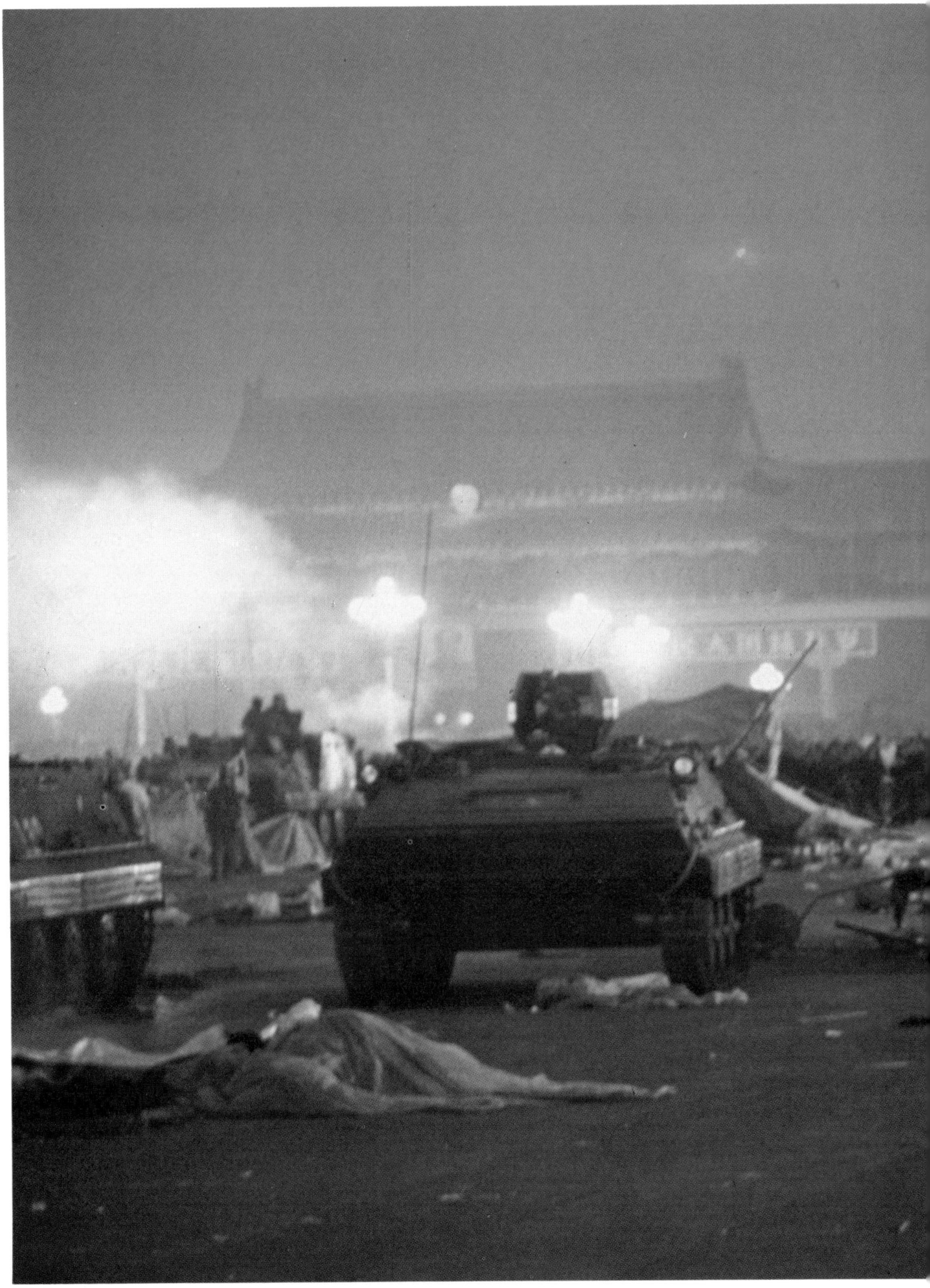

The Tienanmen Massacre

1. Red armor smash tents, crushing students. (Magnum Photo Agency)

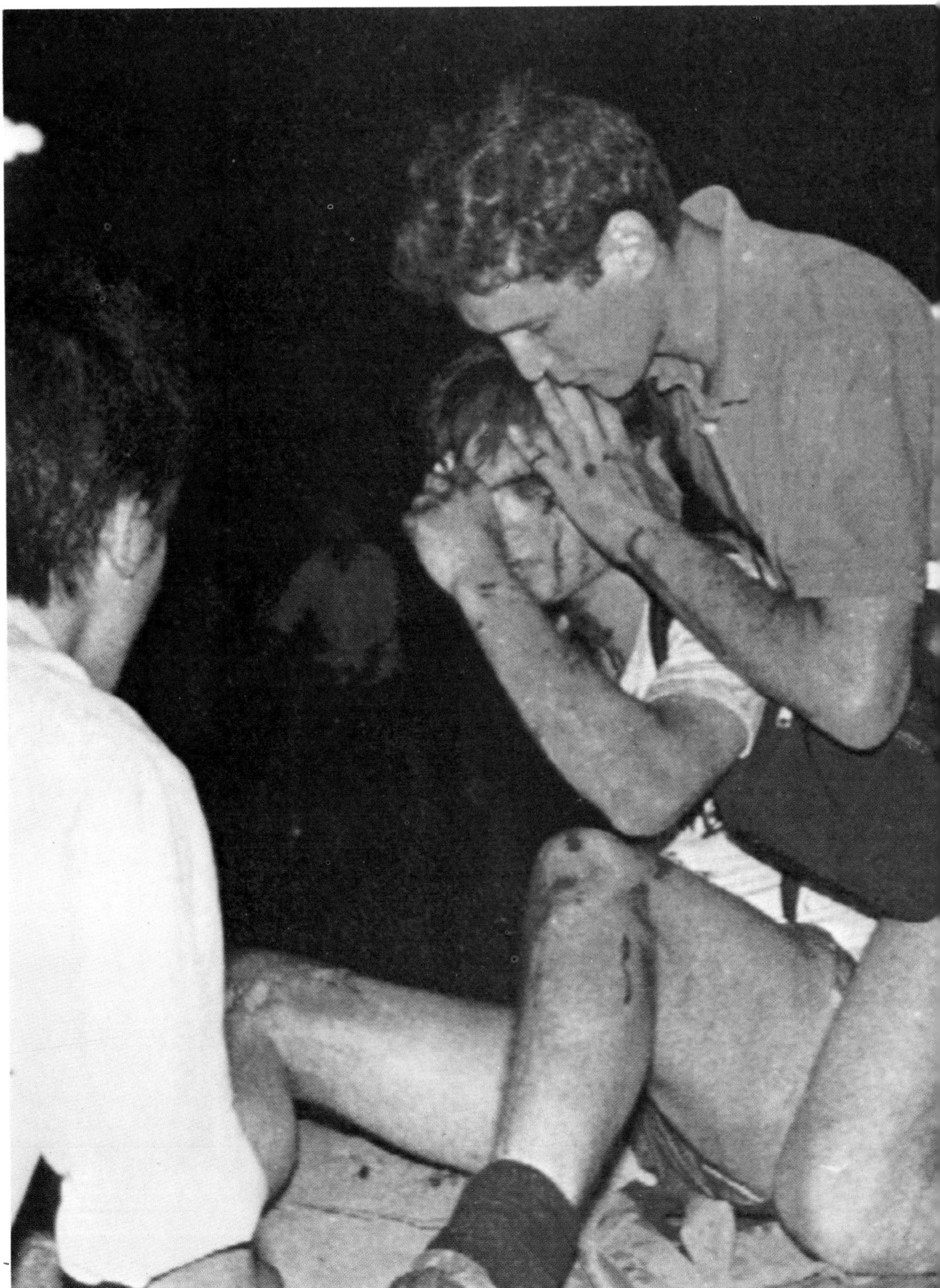

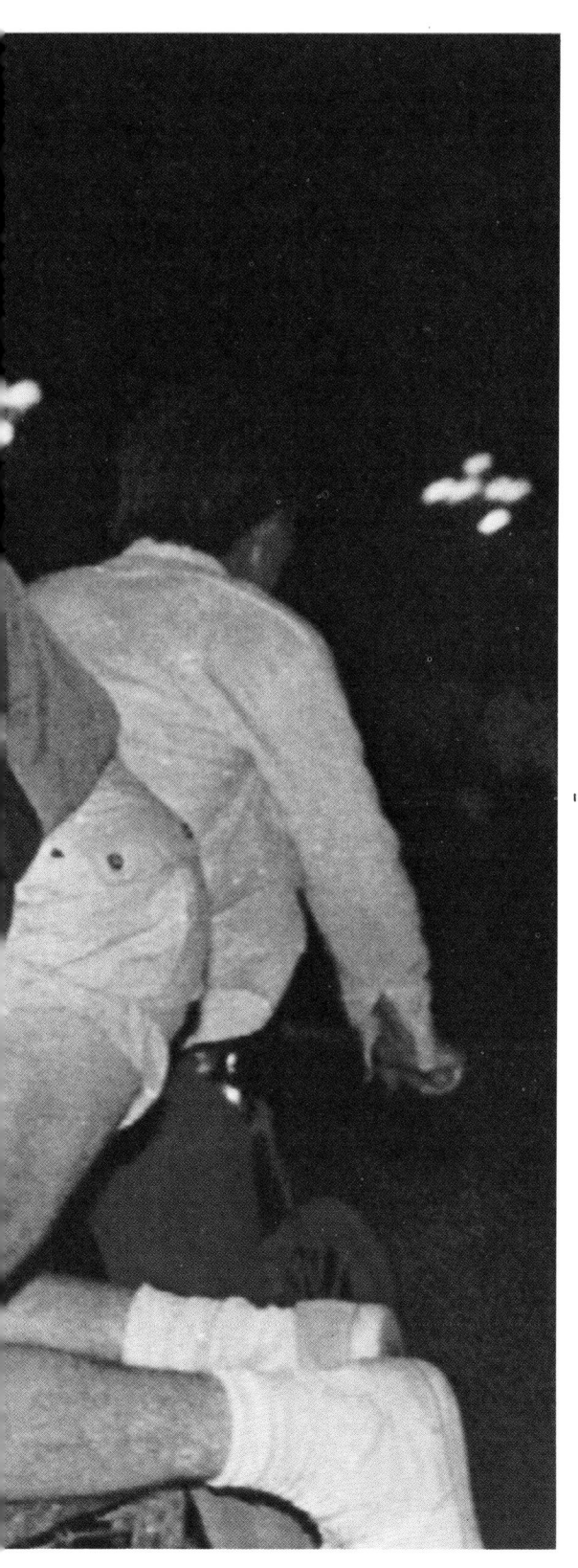

1. Blood-smeared worker's wounds are a red badge of courage. (AP)
2. Foreign reporter was a casualty in onslaught by Red Army. (AFP)

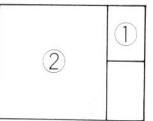

48

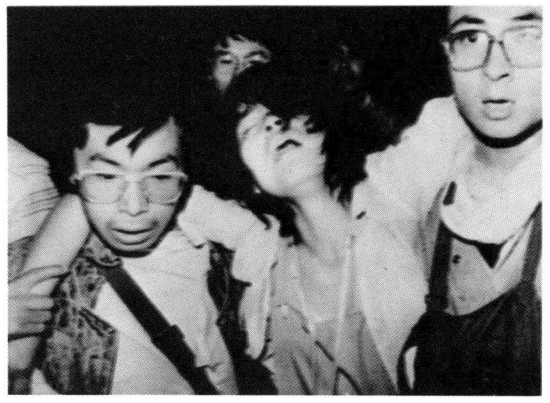

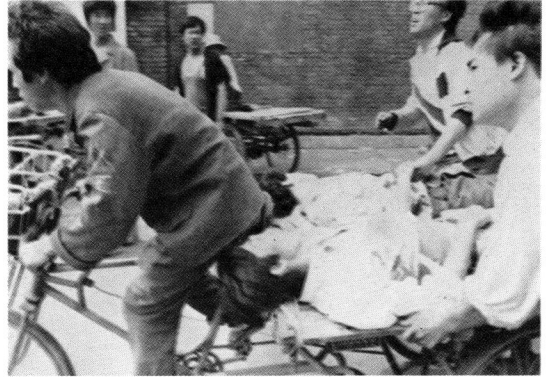

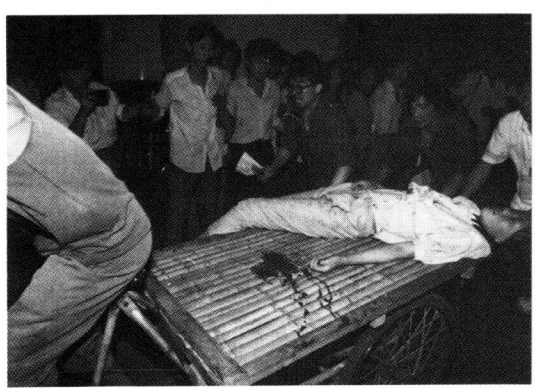

1. A Chinese woman shot by troops at Tienanmen Square. (Reuters)
2. Wounded protesters hauled from Square on carts. (AP)
3. Residents cart away victims of Communist gunfire. (Reuters)
4. Men, women, children fell before army bullets, tanks. (AFP)
5. Many innocents died before they could reach hospitals. (AFP)
6. Students crushed like broken dolls on their broken bikes. (AP)

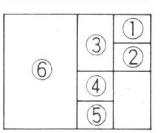

50

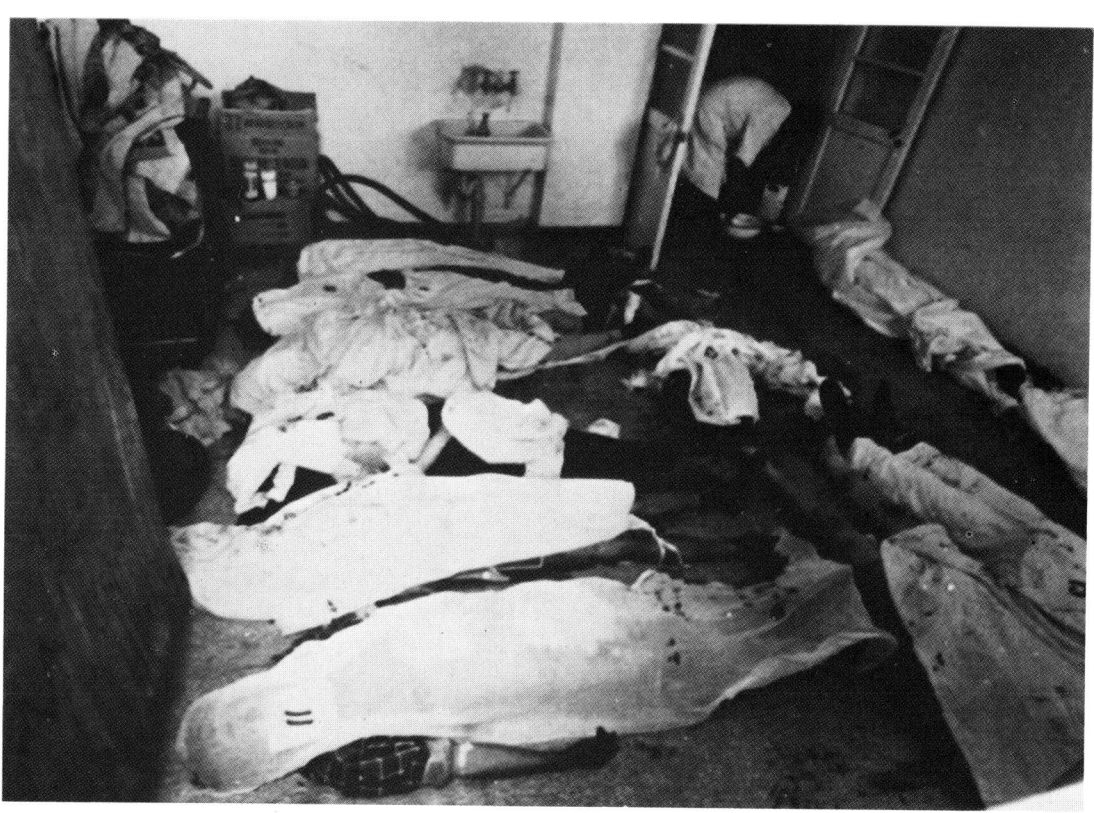

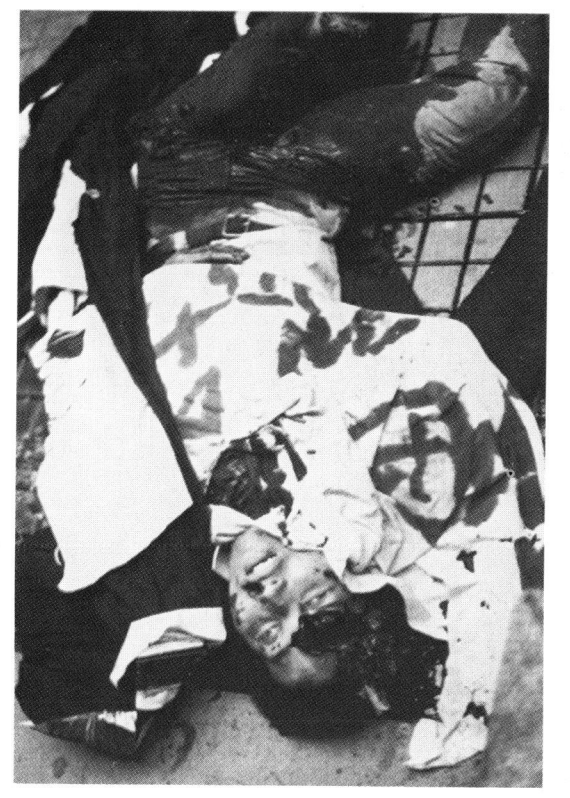

1. Shrouded victims of Tienanmen massacre in temporary morgue. (AP)
2. A student's blanket continues his protest, even in death. (AFP)
3. A crushed bike, a protruding foot, stunned faces. June 4. (AFP)

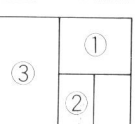

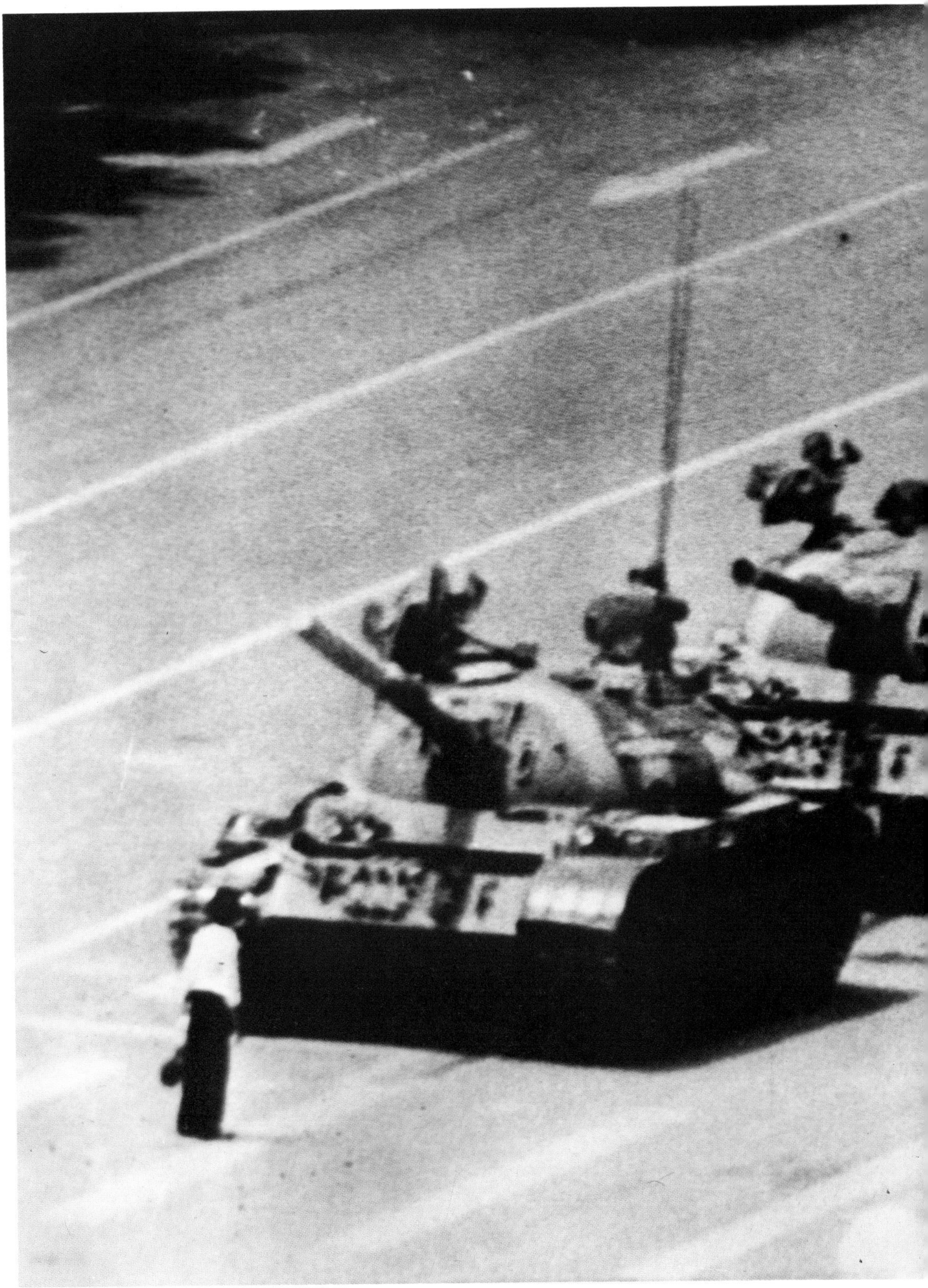

1. Conquerors of unarmed students guard Forbidden City. (Reuters)
2. Behold him, single in the field, tearfully facing a column. (AP)

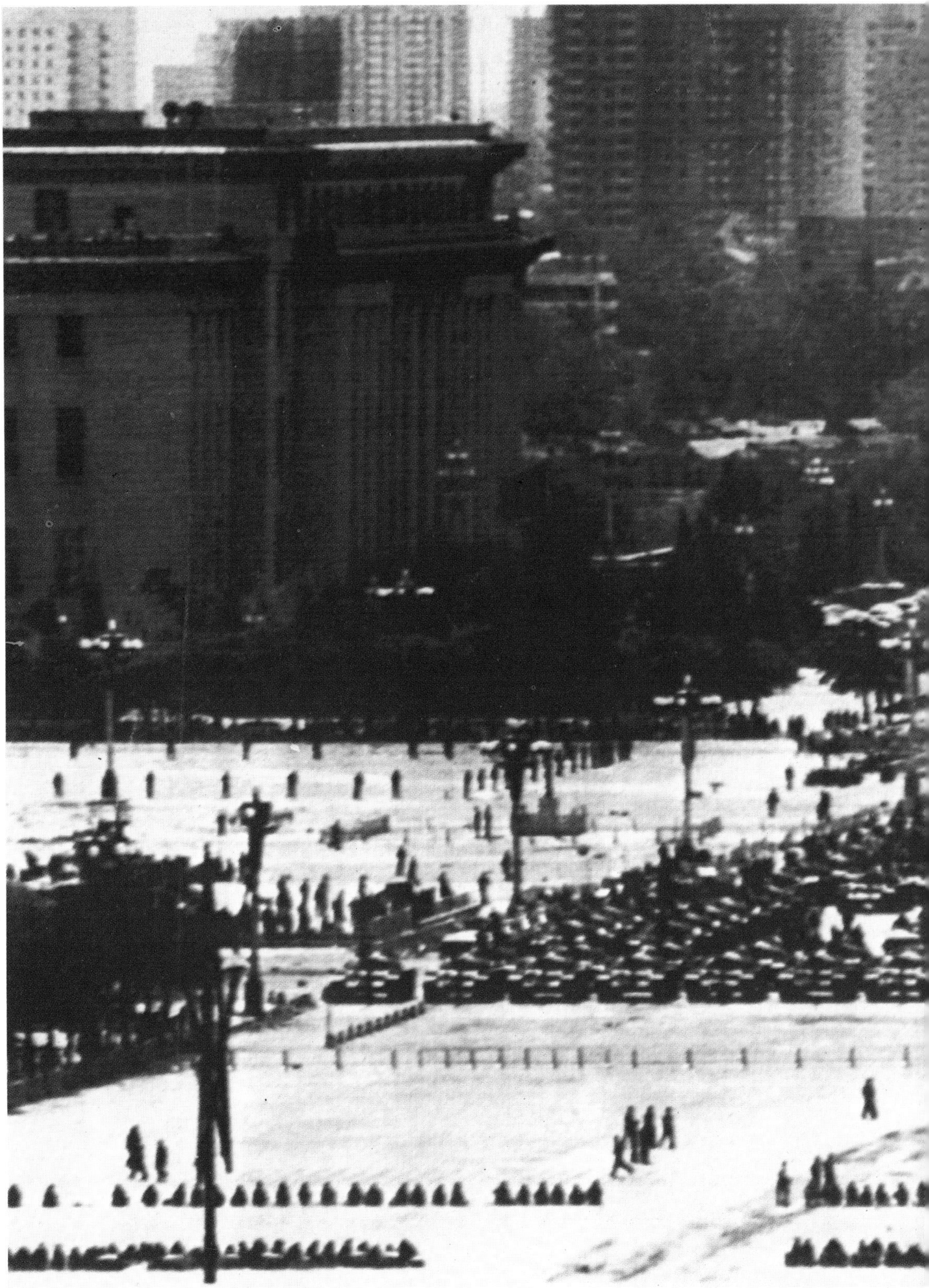

1. Remains of a man, woman, boy or girl squashed by a tank. (AFP)
2. Sea of "People's Army" tanks that crushed the people. (Reuters)

56

1. Idealists: ROC founder Sun Yat-sen. Student leader Wu'er. (AFP)
2. Intellectual Prof. Fan Li-chih took refuge in US Embassy. (AP)
3. Ching Hua University scrolls mourn dead of Tienanmen. (Reuters)
4. Student leader Chai Ling, eloquently pleads for justice. (AFP)

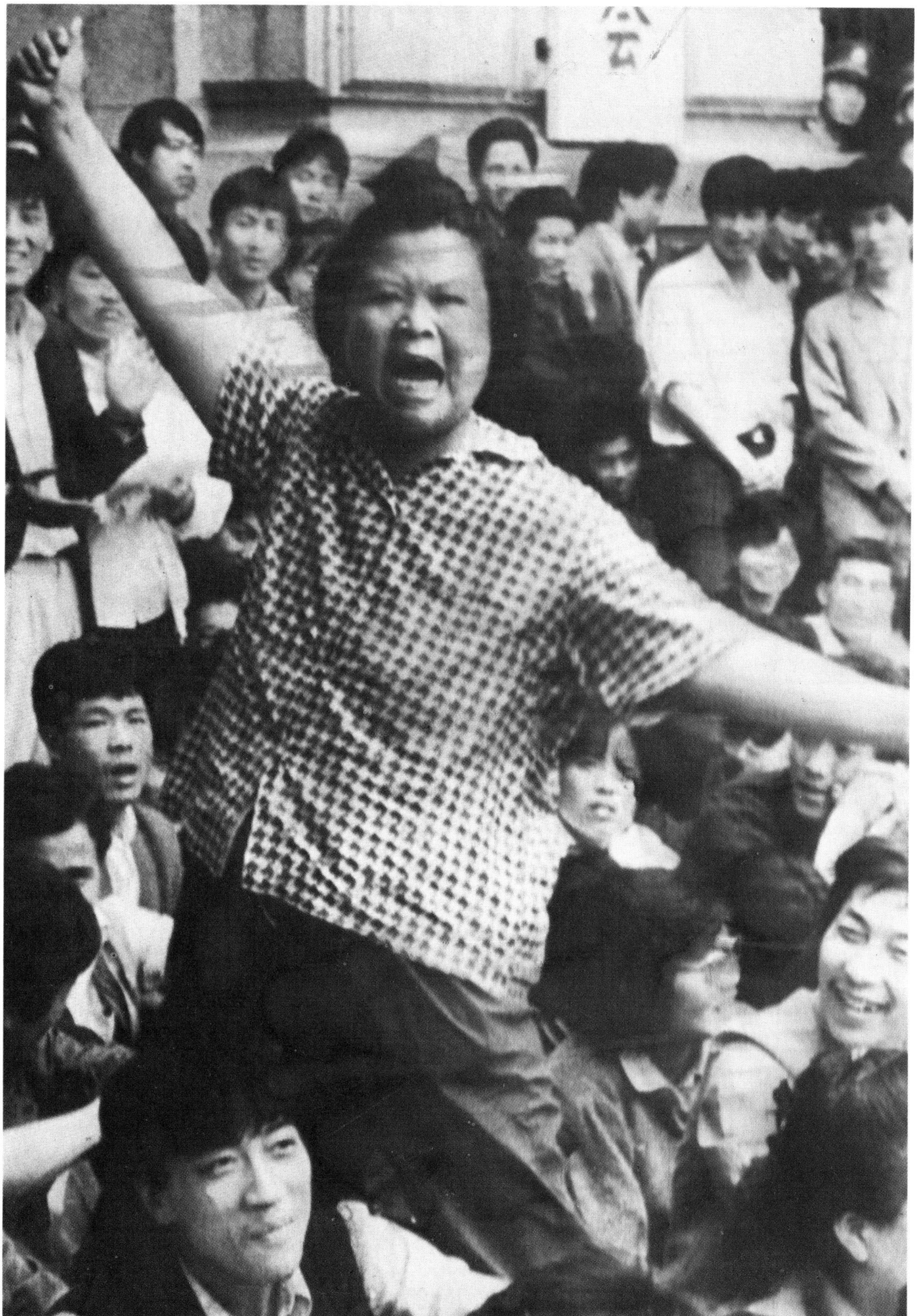

1. Communist consulate duo ask asylum in San Francisco. (Reuters)
2. Forty-thousand Shanghai protesters take to streets. (Reuters)
3. Shanghai woman tells world she supports students. (Reuters)

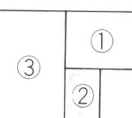

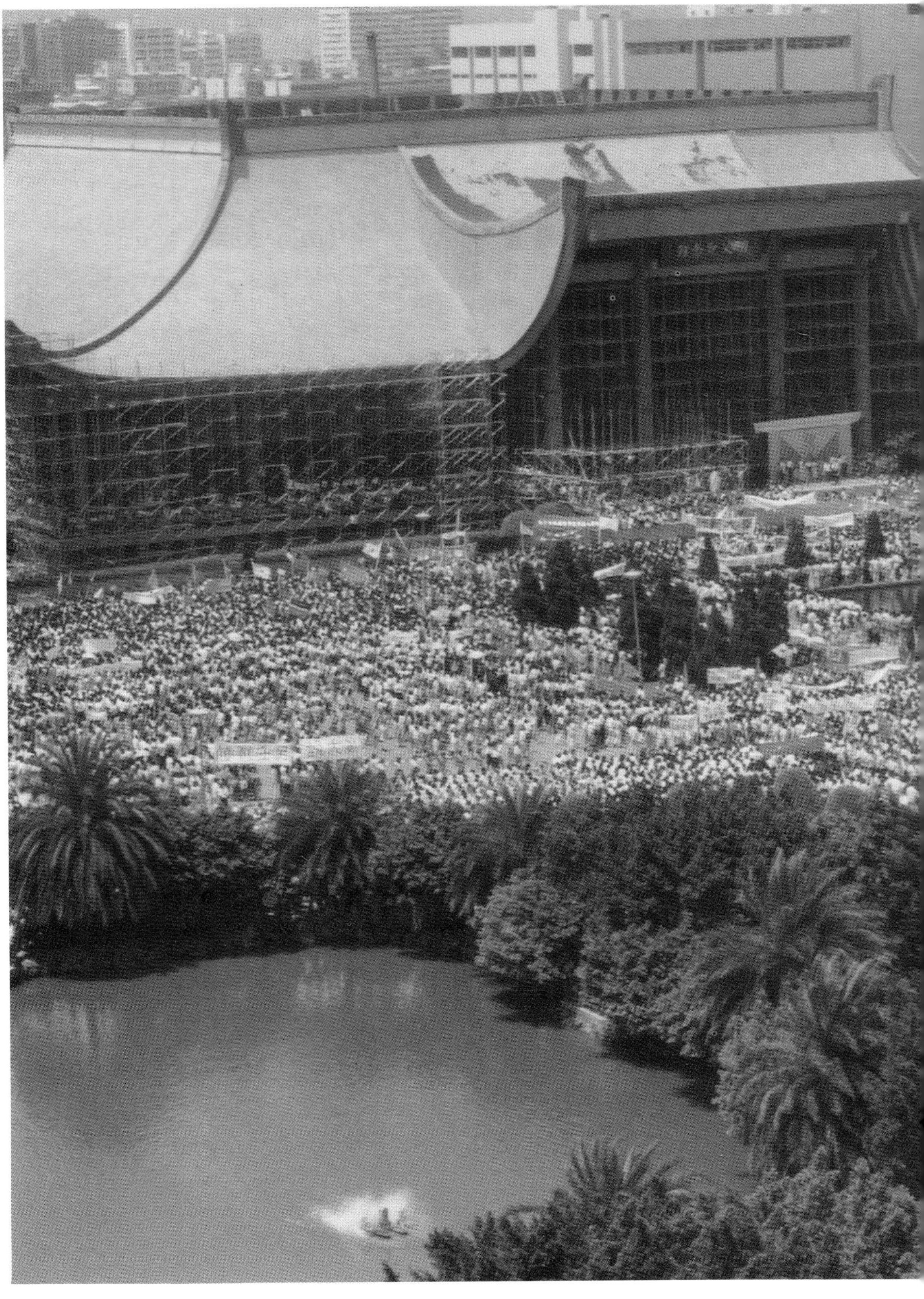

Support from ROC and Abroad

1. Taiwan residents gather at Sun Yat-sen Memorial Hall to protest killing. (Tang Ken-li)

兩岸對歌

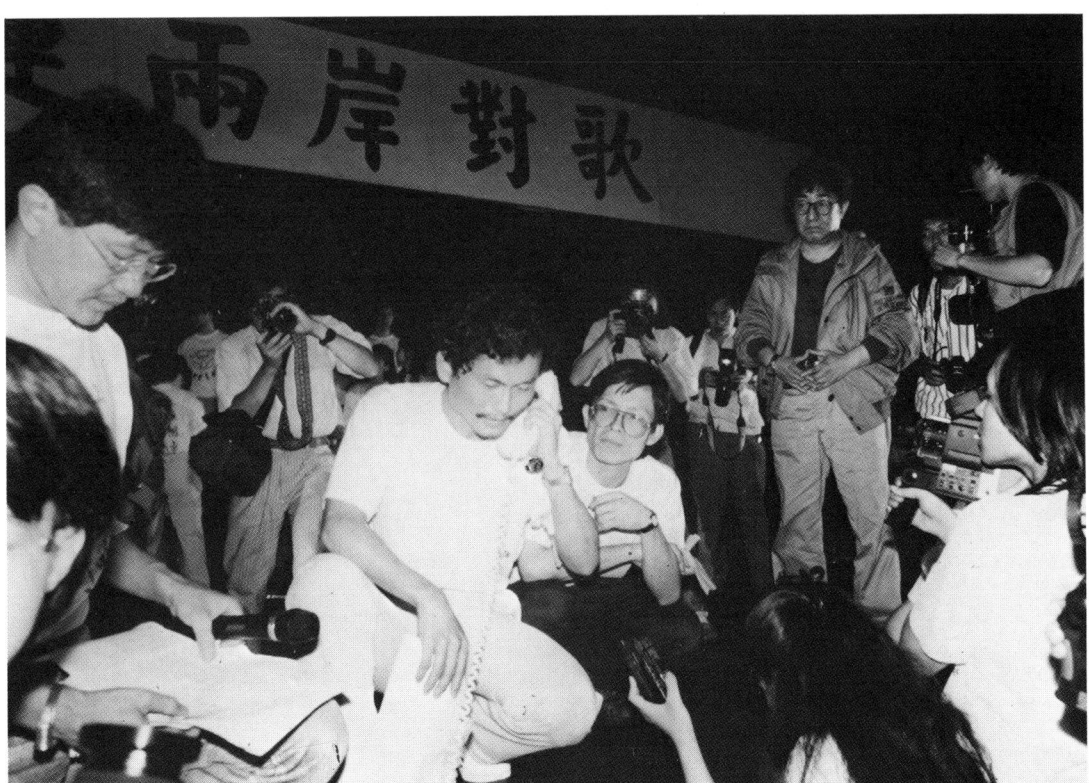

1. Taiwan residents sign vows of support in blood. (Tang Ken-li)
2. ROC papers tell all, float to mainland on balloons. (Tang Ken-li)
3. Taiwan residents mourn Tienanmen Square victims. (Fu Kuo-pin)
4. Singers gather at Taipei pro-democracy rally. (Tang Ken-li)

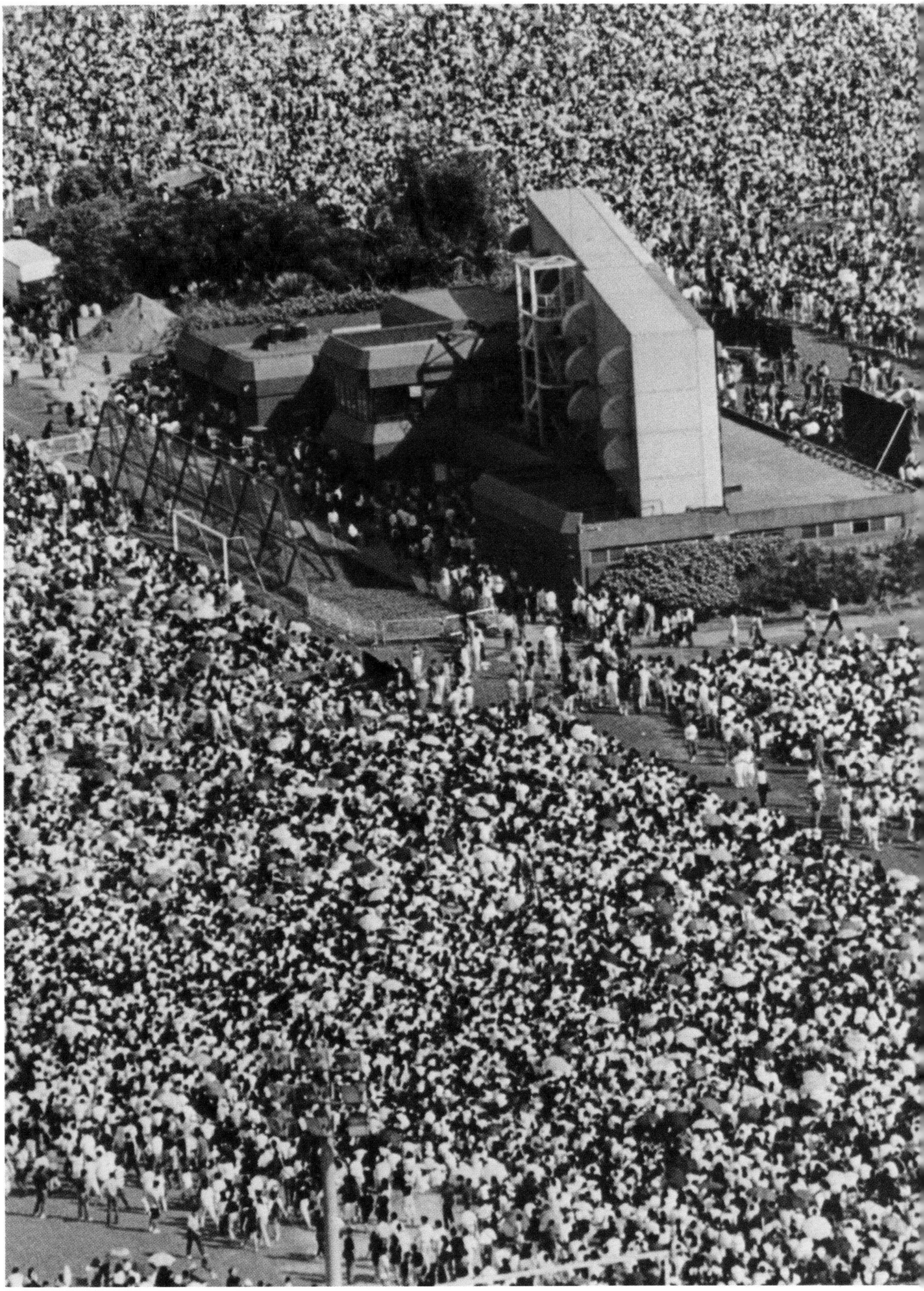

1. Hongkong residents decry Communist massacre.
2. Massive show of support in Hongkong for pro-democracy movement.

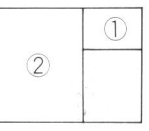

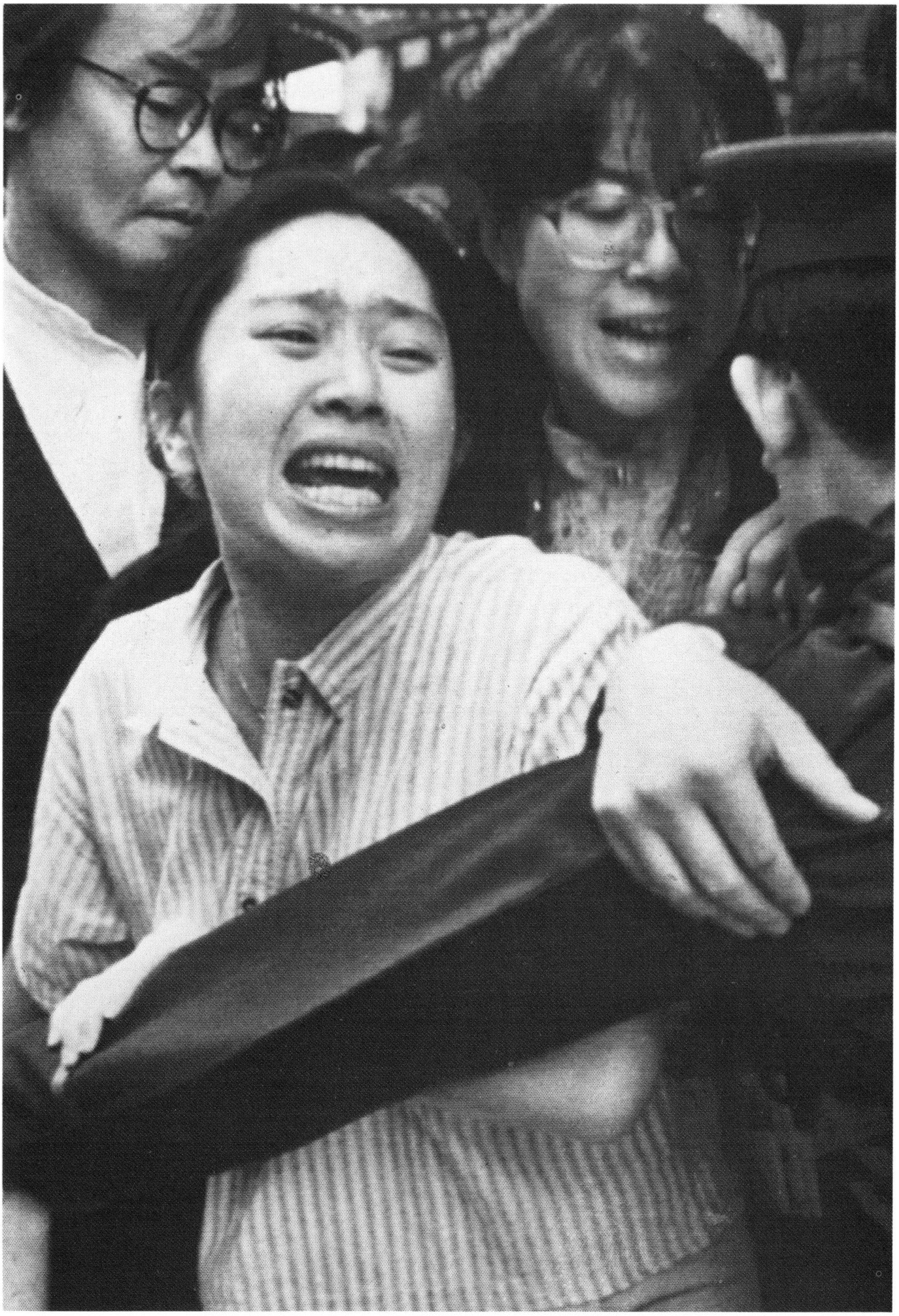

1. Korean overseas Chinese demonstrate against Communist violence.
2. Chinese in Philippines burn effigies of Peking leaders.
3. Thousands of Chinese students mourn at Peking embassy in Tokyo.

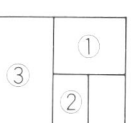

68

1-2-3. Shocked Americans in Washington demand end to "butchery."

69

悼大陸爭取民主...

揭竿而起除暴政
眾志成城...
嘗得心魂在殘軀付劫灰
青燐光不滅基地義軍來
自由火花飛不倦
民主神像...
魂歸天國

奠

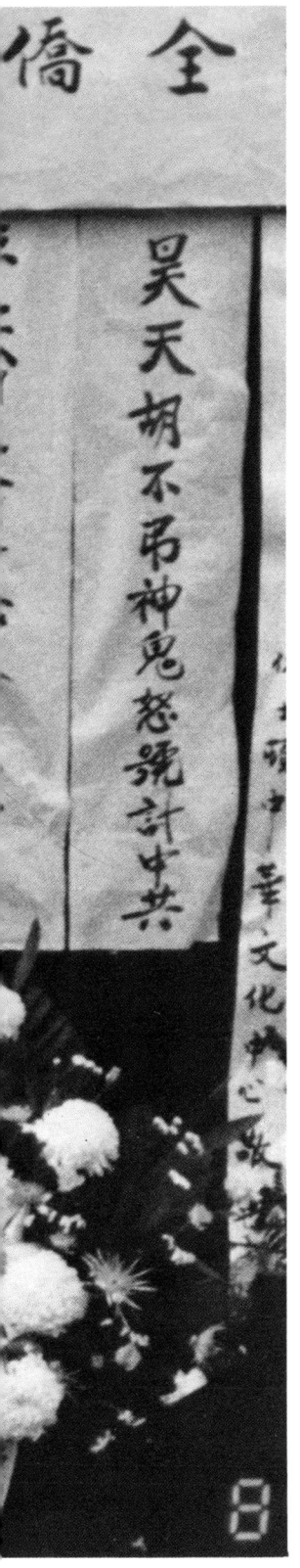

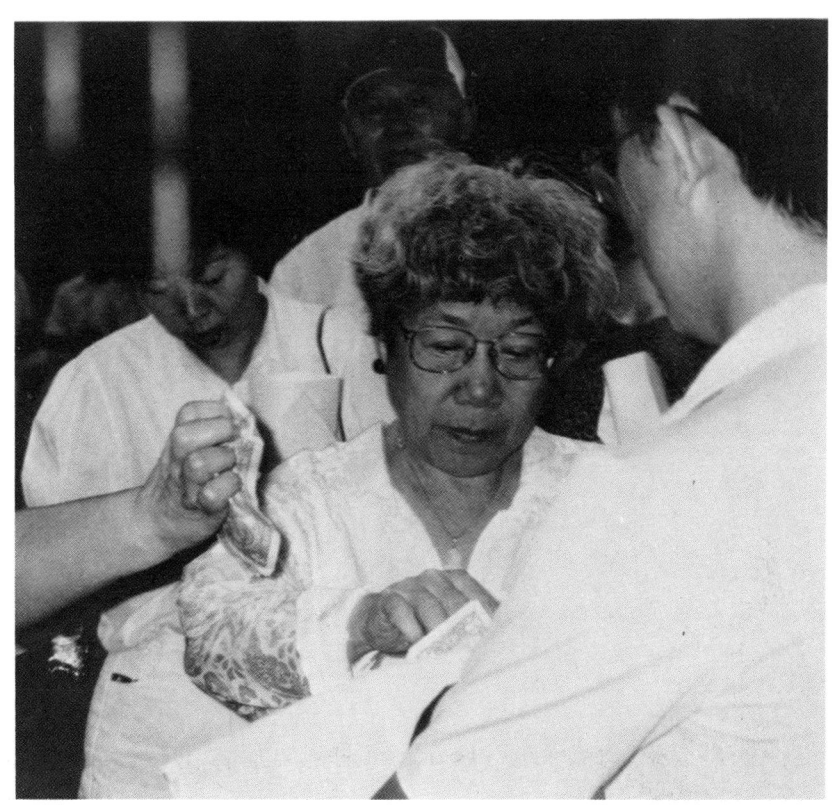

1-2. Texans and Chinese march, mourn and protest in Houston.

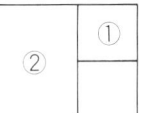

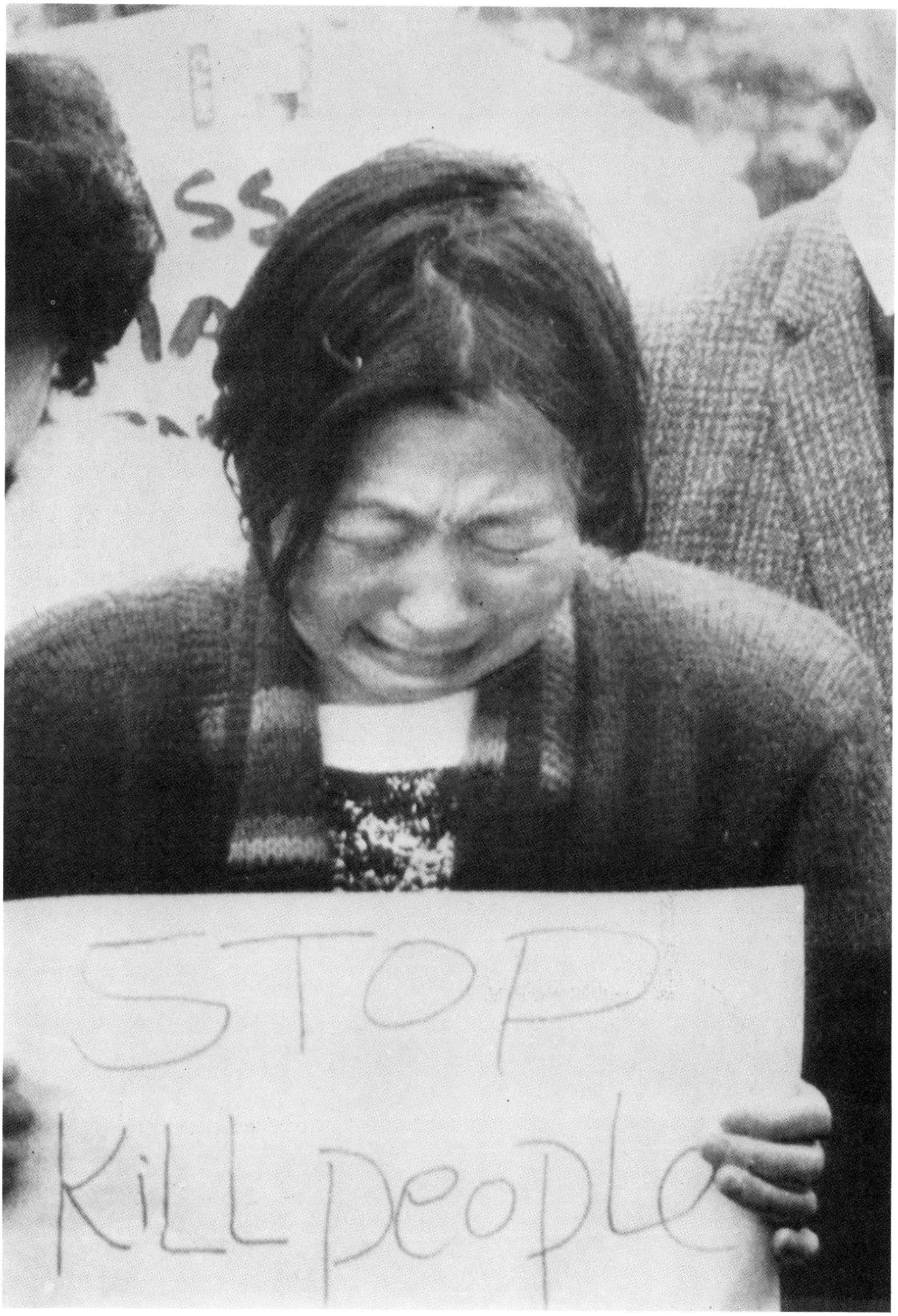
STOP
KiLL people

1. Mainland Chinese students march and cry out in France. (AFP)
2. Chinese Communist embassy in Moscow is besieged. (AFP)
3. Mainland student in Australia pleads for students. (Reuters)

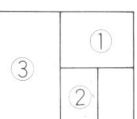